Jeremy Hooker was born in 1941 and grew up in Warsash near Southampton, and the landscape of this region has remained an important source of inspiration. Many of his poems were written in Wales, where he has lived for long periods of his life, and now lives in retirement. His academic career has taken him to universities in England, the Netherlands and the U.S.A. and he was Professor of English at the University of Glamorgan before his retirement. As well as his many collections of poetry, including a *Collected Poems* from Enitharmon, Hooker is also well-known as a critic and has published selections of writings by Edward Thomas and Richard Jefferies, as well as studies of David Jones and John Cowper Powys, all of them important to his own creative life.

Selected Poems
1965–2018

JEREMY HOOKER

Shearsman Books

First published in the United Kingdom in 2020 by
Shearsman Books Ltd
PO Box 4239
Swindon
SN3 9FN

Shearsman Books Ltd Registered Office
30–31 St. James Place, Mangotsfield, Bristol BS16 9JB
(this address not for correspondence)

ISBN 978-1-84861-707-0

PUBLISHER'S ACKNOWLEDGEMENTS
We are grateful to Enitharmon Press for permission to reprint poems
published in *The Cut of the Light: Poems 1965-2005* and *Scattered Light*;
and to Pottery Press for permission to reprint poems published
in *Under the Quarry Wood.*

CONTENTS

from SOLENT SHORE

from ADAMAH

from ARNOLDS WOOD

from SCATTERED LIGHT

from

THE ELEMENTS

Song of the Ashes

for John Cowper Powys

His ashes sang on Chesil bank,
"Old cheat the worms you chose to go
In fire's sensation, body's final fling,

Not in green villages put cold to bed
With ploughmen in their huts of sward,
Not anchored by a stone.

Where all is strange the senses
Twisting whimper like a clueless hound
And terror whips its own heels raw:

You found a way in what you were.
You have amazed the hump-backed bass
By striking, silver-black, at ambush

In the surf, and played the angler
With his trace of wire. The weaver's spine
Inflicts no pain, for your intelligence

Became the poison and the wound;
Nor can you suffer more the ocean's histories,
Returning sated like a shag to roost.

White Nose and Portland,
Chesil's tide-plucked bow of stones,
Are but one shell whose echo cannot sound

Down shelf on shelf the deep-sea crypt.
Adrift on mountain chains, mid-ocean rifts,
An image of the land they mock,

Where all lives tend back whence they came –
What is so strange as to be born?
Fear fear and in the fire be fire."

So sang calm ashes on the sea,
Dissolving on a tide which they made visible.

Easter at White Nose

i.m. Llewelyn Powys

Over downland, where the field
Of wheat in an arc
Drops into space,
We find the clean-cut lettered stone:
THE LIVING THE LIVING HE SHALL PRAISE THEE

The chalk is a globe bitten
Through its axis, the white line
Of retreating cliffs
Jagged with marks of teeth.
Far up in the salt wind,

Hearing the sea crumple
Mouthing its stones, I could lie
Here like ash if death only
Meant contemplation
Under the gently reddening

Sunlight and salt.
Old atheist, the new corn
Has forced a green way
Through flints to the edge
Of your stone. Like St. Francis

You have stretched naked
On the naked ground, thankful

At Easter for the unholy
Resurrections, and sure
There was no other.

These flints teach the same
Dogma, and the brute wheat
Supports you with its fine green
Shoots; perhaps it is only
A wish almost as old to sense
That I speak to a mind
In the smooth domed hill.

Elegy for the Labouring Poor

1. *The Picturesque*

"There will soon be an end to the picturesque in the Kingdom."
    (John Constable, after the destruction, by fire, of Purns Mill.)

I

The picturesque is always with us.
Paint stiffens but the river swims forward;
Clouds move on and a mill becomes ash,
But the human features stay variable
And the pliant earth defies stasis.
And it is there, in that movement,
As another sky forms and a new generation
Measures the wood or levels the corn,
That the imagination commits itself
To an act that is elegy and salutation:
For what is welcomed – this continuity,
Is also change displacing the self that welcomes.
The carpenter alone commands a permanent living,
Elm perpetual usage. Nothing lasts
But the mortal nature of all that's unique.

II

Near Bishopstone the family tended sheep
And ploughed the flint. There I glimpsed
A tractor fuming chalkdust
And found the fields worked profitably
But empty, smooth and pallid.
I came to a village under the downs
Whose graveyard held few stones –
The rest had ended in town cemeteries
Or been put to sea. Not one
Pushed a pen or was pushed by one.

Why grub in the past
For that life whose work seems fickle as ash?
Not to savour lachrymae rerum, nor toll
The general dirge that the globe goes round,
As the elegist wags a grave skull
Sonorous as a belfry: plough fossil,
Fossil pylon…
But to resurrect from the used land
The life that gave life; to utter it
As it cannot be known in the canvas
Where river and cloud stand fast,
Or in chronicles of the cold law;
As it can only be guessed by the self
Acknowledging change; as it can never be known.

2 *Forefather*

He moves like timber on a swell,
In mud gaiters and clay-coloured cord,
Bent to it, sculpting a furrow.
Mould's his name: James Mould
With shoots in Hants and Wiltshire.
His blunt boot-prints, fugitive

As the cloud at his rear,
Are unseen by the camera that exhumes
Celtic patterns from suave downland.
But the tread's purposeful.

His prayer's a bold harvest;
That the seed will stand up golden,
As an army, as mansions in Portland oolite,
As three loaves weekly.
God's ear is readier than Parliament's
Since He'll ferret in barn, byre and hen house,
Tithe hungry.
                    So he trudges,
Chained by daylight
To the round of a stiff field,
Deaf as yet to saucy agitation.
"For living it is not, but a long starving."

3 *"Gold Fever", 1830*

After nightfall in harvest weather,
Over the lowland clay
Where the axe has opened hearts of oak,
A faint wind moves in the rigging of leaves.
On the quayside at Poole
Limestone waits shipment, and Portland
With its moon-grey scars butts into the sea.
Bored by the company of sheep
White horses gallop on the ridge of chalk,
But the Cerne giant, erect through an aeon,
Dreams of slackening into repose.
– Green man, fathering riches,
Delicate in the turn of a leafy wrist
Or puckish among moon-drunk sheaves,
Subject to none but the turning year,
Now fires in the labourer's veins,

Kindling the brand – and flexes strongly,
In the fist that will quench it,
Musket and shot and the outraged warrant
Of a mastering brain…

No man's lonelier than James Mould
As he wakes with stubble-scored legs
In a rat's refuge of wattle and daub.
At first the mist hangs clammy flags
But vanishes as the sun hardens
White-hot on flint, deadening the hedgerows.
Hunger isolates: however neighboured
In a common circumstance,
The body slogs alone, by rote,
And the jailed brain dulls
Fixed on the single motion – the arcing scythe
Deliberate as the sun at its habitual act.
Thus he swings through the day, a young man
Hard and spare as the grain
Now whispering in heaps,
Bent with his shoulder to the field,
Keeping it moving, glad of the work,
At a Klondyke near Bishopstone.

4 *Captain Swing Fires the Workhouse*

Rag bedding indelibly staled,
Lousy straw crusted with piss –
Tinder for the pyre.

Lit, the flames flicker cleanly,
Like a candle in a turnip skull
The house makes a face in the dark.
The grass slithers with rats.
Then the windows stare out,
Splintering, and the fire explodes.

To a shepherd out on the downs
It's a cauldron fed by the oak,
As it ruins suddenly, lustily,
And the walls wither and the roof falls,
Pounding down timber and stone.
Like a yule log
It flickers on the watchful old.

Where's Swing?
The sergeant barks at his redcoats.
The magistrate chokes on latinate prose.

No one knows.
Not even a score of labourers
Cat-footing it through the underwood;
Among them, James Mould,
Daredevil as a boy again,
Pleased with himself and scared.

5 *The Voyage Out, 1831*

Bladder-wrack swaying in supple knots
Muddies the sunned quayside water.
Each for itself and each self
Viciously alike, the black-headed gulls
Snatch at refuse and their raw cries
Spread in circles, smacking the hulk,
Thinning out where the estuary opens
And the sea absorbs their voice.
But James Mould seeing the ocean
Sees only flint acres
Fought inch by inch, chalkdust rising,
And hears only his ghostly kin
Telling their names in the stunned brain.

When Portland pitches astern
And the last gull's torn shoreward,
Memory stays. The hulk bores on,
Shuddering, and the massive slabs break,
The clean fathomless wells slide open.
And the unbroken space narrows
To an inland patch of fields,
The chalk ridge, the sheep-walk scabius.

For this is purgation: to scour men
By divorcing them from all they know.
But the things they love go with them,
Untouchable, at times ferociously clear.
And what's left pleads after them,
And sours. Places are empty
That nothing but bitterness can fill.
The labourer voyages. The land uses
New methods, new men. But he takes with him
A life belonging to those acres
And leaves as a portion, the emptiness.
Under the downs, in countless sites
Gutted by the exile of their people,
Others will meet this isolation.
They will inherit the emptiness.

Earth Poems

1 *Song of the Earth*

Bring or do not bring your mind's distress.
The seas it foundered in
Are none of mine.

My words are flint, cold to your touch.
They tell I am
What you become.

No tree bore the branch
From which your sick thoughts spin.
There is no vertigo in falling leaves.

Along brain's empty dancing-floor
My small blades creep.
The grass's flood-tide bears you home.

2 *At the Edge*

You will haunt the edges
Becoming more shadowy the more
This world streams past.
Now there is nothing but grassblade
Running into grassblade,
Each a separate wave where the colours flux
Orange into brown. The field is going out
With the autumn tide,
And where you were there is now
Only a cry.

Even a poor eye
Can see clear through the globe
To its Antipodes. All, all,
Like a frail door banging in the wind,
A leaky raft through which the sea springs,
Cannot keep out the other elements.
With faculties so weak
You can reach out to touch the other side of death.

Carrying Hay
for Dafydd ap Griffith

We pass a tin cup
For the gulp
Of water, the splash
On a red back
Gummed with straw,
And through the fingers
Easing the joints
Bitten by string.

Trees in shadow ripen
Like plums out of reach
And the bales swung
From hand to hand
Get heavier, building
The last steep load
On the trailer, until,
Senses half-asleep,
We sway from the bare field,
Each slack link dreaming.

Pietà

"Creep back to the earth thy mother!"

With the greenish pallor
Of an unripe stick, his face
Tilts, staring towards
The still pure planets.

Let him come into you,
Mother with the poisoned womb.

There
for Sue

As sett to badger dark in the warm soil;
As moist places to the secret mole,
As essential darkness to earth itself:
Love, the night surrounds us.
We are the confluence of underground streams.
We grow together and in daylight
Flow out apart, now each in each, remade.

LANDSCAPE OF THE DAYLIGHT MOON

Tench Fisher's Dawn

For J.R.

We are before dawn intruders,
Mesmerised by the quizzical pitch eye
Of the lake's animal presence.
It swallows our words without a ripple,
And where we crept up the grasses
Uncoil, effacing our prints. The close dark
Isolates our human stink like prey.
But when the stars melt out and dawn
Unsheathes the black acres, and the water
Pales, steaming under the risen sun,
We can see the bubbles cluster and burst.
Then, casting out, we're suddenly in touch.

Cwm Morgan

for C.A.J.

Once in late summer
Through oakleaves darkened by an autumn breath
I glimpsed the falling river
Torn to shreds of foam, and fancied
That one fleck of whiteness swiftly gone
Might be the fleeting silk
Of an enchantress in your tales.
Then as I turned away
You smiled, as if to say
Cwm Morgan was your gift to me.
                    I did not know
The autumn was already come
When you would slip from me like foam.

Thomas Hardy Burning Letters

Commonsense does it.
First, bed it down, then rake over
Dry grass, dry sticks: that's the knack –
You don't know there's a breeze
Till it snatches; not too tight, though,
Or the match won't take.
That's it.
       Now the paper blackens,
Wrinkles like dead leaves, stains red
As the flames worm through.
It catches. And the heart blooms. Blooms,
And fails into smoke. The ash settles,
And you die as it dies, consumed.
There's only a pale film left, more delicate than petals.

They're all at it, gumbooted, sentinel,
Forking on weeds, trash, contents of attics.
You can see smoke standing up all over Wessex.

       Here's a man
Has a face only the mirror knows,
Who's watched himself burn there
And outstared the horror.
His pitiless scorched lip twitches.
I wonder, is that for a word
The fire glowed through
Before the heart crumpled,
Or because he sees
Scholars, years after,
Scrabble for ash on their knees.

To the Unknown Labourer

No monument
For time to smear;
No statue
That a man conceives
To trap himself in stone.

Only earth
Where a night's rain
Washed out his prints;
Chalk where his life
Was moulded;
Fields like hands after work,
Rough palms spread.

Nobbut Dick Jefferies

('See'd ye owt on the downs?'
'Nobbut Dick Jefferies moonin' about.')

No one but him
Mooning in a backwater
Of the nineteenth century

We've walked apart from the houses
And here, on the edge
Of a common under pines,
Light in every facet
Dances round his words

Such tenderness
Is unbearable;
The point of a grassblade
On the eyeball

Even from the flowerhead
Of a slender foxtail, a branch
Grows over the earth's side
And he has stopped where it bends
Trying the body's weight
Against the bough's strength

The knowledge
Will not disclose itself,
Nor the world make something
Of him, though the extremity
Starts from its roots.

Birthday

For Sue

When I wake, you are standing
Beside me. In the icy Victorian vase
Decorated with glass-cut fern,
You bring catkins, silver-grey

Pussy willow, and snowdrops.
A fine yellow powders your hand.
It is late March, the cold earth
Is broken and out of darkness

You bear a gift. I marvel, love,
To have been born for this.

Landscape of the Daylight Moon

I first saw it inland.
Suddenly, round white sides
Rose through the thin grass
And for an instant, in the heat,
It was dazzling; but afterwards
I thought mainly of darkness,
Imagining the relics of an original
Sea under the chalk, with fishes
Beneath the fields. Later,
Everywhere upon its surface
I saw the life of the dead;
Circle within circle of earthen
Shells, and in retraced curves
Like finger marks in pale sand,
The print of a primaeval lover.
Once, climbing a dusty track,
I found a sunshaped urchin,
With the sun's rays, white
With the dusts of the moon.
Fetish, flesh become stone,
I keep it near me. It is
A mouth on darkness, the one
Inexhaustible source of re-creation.

from

SOLILOQUIES OF A CHALK GIANT

Matrix

A memorial of its origins, chalk in barns and churches
moulders in rain and damp; petrified creatures swim in
its depths.

It is domestic, with the homeliness of an ancient
hearth exposed to the weather, pale with the ash of
countless primeval fires. Here the plough grates on an
urnfield, the green plover stands with crest erect on a
royal mound.

Chalk is the moon's stone; the skeleton is native to its
soil. It looks anaemic, but has submerged the type-sites
of successive cultures. Stone, bronze, iron: all are assimi-
lated to its nature; and the hill-forts follow its curves.

These, surely, are the work of giants: temples
re-dedicated to the sky god, spires fashioned for the
lords of bowmen:

Spoils of the worn idol, squat Venus of the mines.

Druids leave their shops at the midsummer solstice;
neophytes tread an antic measure to the antlered god.
Men who trespass are soon absorbed, horns laid beside
them in the ground. The burnt-out tank waits beside
the barrow.

The god is a graffito carved on the belly of the chalk,
his savage gesture subdued by the stuff of his creation.
He is taken up like a gaunt white doll by the round hills,
wrapped around by the long pale hair of the fields.

Found Objects

1
A reindeer bone carved
in the reindeer's likeness.
Saddle-quern
Loom-weight
Spindle-whorl.
A chalk phallus.
A lump of chalk
with heavy curves bearing
the image of woman.

2
A necklace with blue beads
of Egyptian faience, black ones
of Kimmeridge shale.
Slingstone
Cannon ball
Cartridge.
A phallus carved on the church wall.
A statuette of the Virgin.

3
A coin worn headless,
with a disarticulate horse.
Cartwheel
Crank-shaft
Flash-bulb.
A bust of the death-god
cast in imperishable alloy.

Flints

They are ploughed out,
Or surface under surface

Washes away leaving the bleached
Floor of a sunken battleground.

Some are blue with the texture of resin,
The trap of a primeval shadow.

Others are green,
A relic of their origins.

The white one is
An eye closed on the fossil.

Worked in radial grooves
From the bulb of percussion

They shed brittle flakes.
The core with its brutal edge

Shaped the hand.

The Age of Memory

It is over three hundred years since the churchwarden
paid a carpenter three and tenpence for converting the
maypole into a town ladder.

The puritan is a good toolmaker. He contracts his
workforce from the boozy remnant whooping in the ring.

Even a backwater is shaken by purposeful tremors,
when it empties. Afterwards, the place is greener. The
native god is exposed for the first time.

If the god is a spectacle, he is no longer blind. In the
scheme of things he becomes guardian of the dead. He is
invested with memory. The insignia of office is an
invisible globe.

Totem

Where are the giant's people?
They have followed the mole
Under mounds. The Dance
Is a ring of stones.

Soon there will be nothing
But a breeze gathering dust
Over pale fields, a maze
Of ditches scored on the hill,

Unless a man stand naked
Of all bur imagination.
Let him discover me.

I rise through him
Or lie here and wait,
Scratched in the chalk.

The Giant's Boast

I was before Christ, and I remember
The saurian head of my begetter,
I conceived these words at my creation,
When you traced your shadow on the stone.

I was before Moses, and his fury
Returned me to the elements,
From which I am remade.

I have walked with my ribcage naked,
When the strong man dug his grave.
I have contemplated the skeleton
Under the flesh of all things,
And I gave to the holy waters
A natural potency.

The smoke from a wicker basket
Was sweetest to my nose;
For I have levelled and engendered
Multitudes, and I do not answer
To a single name.

No man understood me
Who called me brutal, and no woman
Who called me kind.
Mothers and daughters worshipped me.
I worshipped with my body
The naked ground.

The Giant's Shadow

I am the giant who carries a giant
On his back.
This is my comrade.
Is he alive or dead?

I stoop and cry out,
Let go, let go.
When I look up
The shadow hangs over me
With crossed wings . . .
Impure fancies, how they breed
In the sludge
Of a standing mind!

Do you imagine the dead stop in their graves?
Stones of the abbey that vanished
Are mounted on my spine.
This is history,
When the mind is an open grave.

You are sunlight,
You are darkness,
Green god.
The rest is illusion.
Illusion with talons hooked through my bones.
It is an anchor
From the bottom of the sea,

It is fixed in the floor of the sea
Like an axe-head fast in a skull.
If I could move it, the world would shift.

How heavy the shadows are!
I wrestle with them all day long,
Fingers clutched round my cold stave.

What Is a Giant Made of?

I have seen myself
Standing defiantly
Apart from the hill,
And I have seen,
Through earth's tissue
And a sky
Without foundation,
The daylight moon,
Brittle as a chalk fragment,
Reflecting my disdain.

What is a giant made of?

There is a clump
Of flowering blackthorn
Spattered with the dung
Of rooks: these, too,
Are the giant,
These white flecks.
There my eye sleeps
With its mirrors turned
To the wall of my skull,
And beneath me
I feel the grass rise
And fall, like the slow
Deep breaths of a giantess.

A Chalk Pebble

This is perfect:
A chalk pebble,
Smooth and round,
Like an egg
With the foetus
Of a giant
Curled inside.

When I touch it,
My hand crumbles.
The hill is a fine cloud
Whitening the Cretaceous sea.

Starfish, urchin, sponge,
I have become many:
We do not trespass here,
Composed on the white floor.
We are not foreign to this ground.

Who is the saurian
Tyrannizing the shallows,
Smashing a trackway
Through the new green trees?
His familiar,
Disproportionate head
Is small and mean.

The giant turtle is in its element,
Housed on the summit
Of low white hills.
The dead sponge mingles
With alchemic water
For the slow formation
Of a perfect stone.

Dawn

There is a moment
No one sees,
When earth is formed
In the image of neither
Mist nor light.

Grey flowers grow
On the giantless hill,
Over the untouched graves.
Sleeper and sleepless lie
Without a name.

Colour breaks and this day
Is one of the millions,
Bloodred, gold, with a streak
Of unearthly green
Like the eye of a god.

Dawn is perfection
Of a kind. Now I wake
To the unfinished act
And the dead lie complete
For ever, under their names.

Chalk Moon

How it leeches the mind,
When a daylight moon rises
Like a piece of the hills.

There is no darkness here;
The living are so remote.
Even the club feels powdery,
Crushed in my hand.

The sea has withdrawn far out;
Streams cannot reach it.
They die of thirst
In a landscape picked to the bone.

When the wind blows
My breath tastes of dust.

Devil

Who was the goat upon hindlegs
Who tickled with a whiskery thigh
The hairless monk?

When the young friar drowsed
I drew with his goosequill in the margin
Pictures of beasts and birds.

He saw a devil to castrate,
Initialled in God's name between my legs,
Jehovah Destroyed This.

Though weather rubbed it out,
This was God's patent for the age.

I am the pupil of the eye,
Diminished by a cool, bored look.

Aborigine

Streams dig with their flints.
Chalk rises through stubble
Like a moon. From this page
I learnt my name.

Everything refers me back
In time. Chalk words. Flint words.
The chalk are porous, and crumble.
The flint are hard.

I am bound to the place
By its language.
I was taught to speak
In such metaphors.

When I am dead the language
Will shed me. Till then
It takes something of me
Wherever it goes.

Yellowing Moon

The rotted flints alone
Are motionless. They lie
In half-light, blue scars
Touching, under the barley.

Hardly a patch shows white.
Shadow softens the glare
Of tracks. These are nights
Of the yellowing moon.

Now fire-tints melt
Enclosures, run fields together
In one broad curve
Of ripening grain.

A pigeon flaps away;
Heat-haze resolves it
In a dozen yards
Into a burr of energy.

Nothing is self-contained.
There is no standing apart,
Of tree, or barn, or man.
I am possessed like a single stalk.

Elegy for the Giants

Scorn broke them; they softened,
Mouldering like touchwood.
An effigy found in an attic,
Lugged out to be burnt,
Was once the molten god.

Beggared Herakles became a clown
And as the clodpole with a stave,
Beelzebub, invited blows
And laughter. They bragged
And bluffed and roared,
Jaws gored with rouge,
Exalting some boy-hero
By their fall.
Like Ysbadaddan,
All were well shaved.

Others turned to stone.
They wear grey habits
With an austere dignity.
They are upright, with ascetic faces.
They have fallen and do not plead.

The Spring

Let there be peace between us,
Tortured god.
Like a lesser sun,
The light of your church
Once cast my shadow.
I sprouted horns
Like a Lord of Beasts.

I am no longer strong
In my strength;
And you, no longer strong
In your weakness,
Can you accept this water,
Once sacred to me,
That your blessing cursed?

Novelty

You call me old,
But to the wind I am
A novelty, and to the rain
No more than the shallows

Of a man-shaped stream.
As for the earth, I barely
Exist. It is early yet
To speak of extinction,

Though we each keep
A different time. If,
To survive, I am less than
Human, my image forms

Between you and the ground.
Alone, I cut a feeble figure.
Only admit we belong
To each other, and begin.

Solstice

Is the poppy afraid
Of its redness?
I am not a dry leaf
That flares to nothing.

Roots drink at my side.
Chalk absorbs my warmth.
And still I am replete,
Blood-ripe.

The facets of every flint
Glow red. No surface

Remains unkindled
To reflect my stare.

All day sun passes
Through me.
I am burned on the hillside
With its brand.

Prayer in Winter

Give me courage, hunter,
When energy has bled down
To the roots and the moon
Is a chalk pebble hurled
Into the sky, when rain
Turns dust to sludge
And the wind hacks my groin.

Give me the courage
Of your slow retreat
From the frozen springs, following
The signs of reindeer and bison.
When life retreats, let me
Follow the signs.

from

SOLENT SHORE

New Year's Day at Lepe

Set out on a morning of white thaw
smoking between oaks, Hatchet pond so still
it might have been frozen
except for the long slender rods
as if painted on its dark blue glaze.
Saw nothing of the *Private, Keep Out*
notices of semi-feudal estates,
but cock pheasants in brown fields
of sharp-edged clods, poking out their necks.
Then the small rusty bell of the shingle
tinkled and grated as it dragged,
a shadowy tanker bared its round stern
and Marchwood power station exhaled
a breath which the sun tinged pink;
but of all things none seemed newer
than gravel with its sheen of fresh oranges
at the water's lip. Brought away that,
and an old transparent moon
over the Island, the delicate industrial sky
blue-grey as a herring gull's back,
and a small sunny boy running beside
the great wet novelty shouting *wasser, wasser.*

Paintings
for my father

Avon weir pouring

suspended, the race
brushed still, river
and sky, shadow,
sunlight and trees rushing

enclosed, opening
the house on water.

Slow Boldre,
slower Stour:
gold shallows;
dark, Forest pools

or where they run
dammed – white whorl
of an eddy, or flow
barred – green, brown

pass from seclusion
of leaf and earth,
blue oils spreading
contained:

Christchurch fluid
on the wall,
the shore at Keyhaven
where an easel stood.

Rat Island

1
With first light
The bearings surface.

From Tennyson's memorial
To Sway tower,
From Jack in the basket
To Fawley,
Point after point
Rises on time.

I mark them,
Borne back
On a freshening wind.

The sea completes the circle.

2
There are no rats;
Except at high spring,
No island.

Only a relic
Of the late defences
Harbouring
Mud-dwellers.

Part of the shore
That curves away,
Keen as a tern's wing.

3
I have stayed long enough
Casting a shadow.

    Let it be
As it is
When a tern dives
And on the blue sky
In the water, between
The smooth hulls
Of mudbanks,
The wind casts waving lines.

Pitts Deep

Over Abbey ploughland
On a brown, winter day
Of Cistercian calm,
No one will go observing
The silver bell mouth of the sky,

Or cross the manorial path
Into oakwoods descending
Almost to the water –
Except, perhaps, two friends
With a bottle of cheap wine
Who walk in confessional mood
Where forest ponies also go,
Trampling soiled, silky weed
On mudbanks and quills
Of bleached salt-grass,
Sowing a trail of droppings
On the stilled shore.

Friend with a Mandolin
for Jim Insole

Singer with a mandolin,
Pluck from the smoke
Of a humdrum bar
The raw defiant strings
Of Mountjoy and Van Diemen's Land,

Let the bland south
Hear the blues.

From the cradle
Twanging in your hands,
Pick Café Mozart.

At closing time, we'll sit out
On the shingle drunkenly
Amazed to think of France,
So far away, still serving wine.

By Southampton Water

The water is bottle green, with a salt crust
And an unmistakable flavour of sewage.

A tarred gull floats past; an orange box
And the helmet of a marine; a glove
With the hand still in it.

Going home,
The view from Totton flyover
Makes me gape
Even now.
             The river's wedge broadens
Seaward; a dream of cranes swims in haze;
Smoke from the power station silvers the blue.
Everywhere, men I know work under it.
Necessities are unladen and shipped.
That is the root.

Black ribs of a hull in the mud.
'It's a Viking,' my parents said.

'Viking': the word's a skeleton of spars
With sky through it,
Sticking up from blue-grey mud.

As the song goes:
                When the tide is out at Totton
                The stench is something rotten…

True; but I cannot imagine sea without it;
Without gumboot-sucking ooze;
Small green crabs sidling by old green posts;
Without tugs and the giant Queens.

At night, crossing to Hythe,
The water squirms with ideograms.

I could spare a life trying to decipher them.

The Water's Edge

In a time between
flying boat and hovercraft,
between stained tanks
through villages, and waves
of Solent City:

in a place over
caved-in paths echoing
the tidal swill,
over windrows of shell
and beaker: here

I return, like sun
on the river's green back
that cannot pierce it,
or remain, like stones
I once threw, working
a blind passage in the mud.

Though waves set hard
along the coast,
and new amphibians
displace the old,
part of me stays
at the water's edge,
greased with use, among
corks, tarred feathers,
bits of boats, tins
knocking against the wall.

Solent Winter

1

Yachts on the leaden estuaries
are wingless, larval.
Leeward of the island
rusty bums of tankers
squat in the swell.
This full-bodied water
bears its trademark in oil.

Now the tides grease a shore
stripped to its working parts.
High over the cranes
Fawley Beacon burns.

2

On short dim evenings
the grey island floats off-shore
like a ghostly berg;
liners are lit up for Christmas
with the stores.

Where Southampton Water forks
the town is grounded
on gravel shoals.
Funnels converge on the centre.
Portholes and windows shine.
The streets trap echoes
of muted horns.

Wires still buzz with messages
from the *Titanic.*
A séance breaks up
when a cabin-boy screams.

On a Photograph of Southampton Docks

for Brian Maidment

Blinding silver on grey,
a suntrack points deep
into this average morning.
All is ready for work:
launches at their moorings,
small tubs off the pierhead,
warehouses; and above all
the cranes, these flying high
or with pulleys dangling,
those far back, more spidery.
No, it is not their function
to please the eye.
Yet they do – more so
for the common goodness
of their function, for grace
extra to a working world
that neighbours sky and water,
drawing from all
some ordinary tribute;
for that reason too,
more beautiful, as they say:
like birds, like dancers.

Floating-Bridge

You look for
a good haul
in green, milky water
where chains slide over reels.

Is it, perhaps, the sludge
of nostalgia, or the unseen
seen too narrowly?

Whatever it is,
the chains go deep.

From a Pill-Box on the Solent

On a day of ripped cloud,
Angled light, wind against tide,
I am tempted to begin
The story of my life.

Waves come from far off,
Through the gap they have made,
Between Purbeck and Wight.

Surf booms in the pill-box,
Rattles the shingle,
Folds over it, unfolds,
Laying it bare.

Let it blow sand or salt.
Here at least I tread without fear
Of unsettling dust.

Solent Shore

Where the shoreline ends
At the horizon, the far sky's
Pronged with orange flames
From the refinery.

Today the clouds bear east,
Forming a broad, shadowy space
Of dark green mudlands,
Staked out with old stumps,
With rows of masts along
Estuaries and creeks.

It might be almost any time,
As one slow hulk of cloud
Lags to the west, mirrored
Like an oil slick off the Needles.

Rice Grass

(Spartina Townsendii)

Praise one appearing
lowly, no man's rose,
but with roots far-reaching
out and down.

Give homage to a Spartan cross,
native and American,
hardier and more adaptable
than those; nearly a newcomer
but one that, by staying put
has made itself a home;
also a traveller east and west.

Celebrate the entertainer
of sea aster, sea lavender,
thrift and nesting gulls;
lover of mud and salt;
commoner and useful colonist,
converter from ooze
of land where a foot may fall.

Mary Rose (1545)

Sunk by her own guns
cannoning to leeward,
gunports open to the sea.

The King he screeched
like any maid:
'Oh my gentlemen.
Oh my gallent men.'

All over. The cry of mun,
the screech of mun, Oh Sir,
up to the very heavens.

The very last souls I seen
was that man's father
and that man's.

Drowned like rattens,
drowned like rattens.

Where the Gravel Shelves

From the shallows of sleep,
Out where the gravel shelves,
The sharp white rocks passing,
The shore, the open sea, passing
Taller the white rocks,
Further the shore, closer
But less attainable
The open sea…
You, chin above water,
Always afraid of the undertow,
The firm foot slipping, you
Whose strongest emotion was fear
Approach now the dreamless, deep
Stillness, silent as a ship's bell
Stopped with a bell of mud.

Prospect of Boldre Church

Raised above oaks
Above a full river.

Once the living
Of William Gilpin.
Now his quiet mansion.

He hopes to rise
In God's good time.

Dim, coloured light
Stains the sanctuary,
The lettered stones
Charged with patience.

Things that seem misplaced
Catch the eye
Irresistibly,
Even as it bends:

H.M.S. Hood;
The Book of Remembrance,
Names illuminated
Of the able-bodied.

The head inclined to bow
Remains unshocked,
But cold; observes

St. Nicholas
Overlooking benches
Carved with her crest;
Pictures the sea

Outside the frame: colder
For fires quenched in a flash,
For steel made a harrow
Useless on the ocean bed;

Even here, enclosed
Above oaks above
A full river, the sea
Open, spirited shipless.

At Osborne House

Under cedar and ilex,
On lawns to us *verboten,*
Convalescents watch us,
From coach and car,
Mobbing their repose.

         His too,
Albert of Saxe-Coburg's,
His bay of Naples, his
Renaissance villa,
His evergreens, which,
After more than a century,
Cast longer and darker shadows.

If it were quiet, if
I could attend,
I might imagine
Innumerable salutes,
         the waterway
Busy with despatches,
Screwed and churning,
Hatched with white, cross lines.

Among her many possessions
The Empress of grief
Becomes her statue,
                    marble
Among marble and horn,
Silver and ivory, mahogany and teak.

Here is India, here
St Petersburg
On a vase of Nicholas I,
Here Kaiser Wilhelm
Of the waxed aspiring moustache.
                         The musical-box
Plays a march from *Tannhäuser.*

She is Britannia;
To her Neptune entrusts
The Command of the sea.

The finish is perfect,
A spectacle,
Complete –
Like the royal children's marble limbs.

I would rather look out,
Down terraces of statuary,
Over woods of oak and beech,
Elms dying or dead,
To the blue Solent,
Spithead,
The tower blocks of Portsmouth.

The young Queen bathing
For the first time
Ducked her head:
'I thought I should be stifled.'

On the balcony with Albert
She heard the nightingales.
Here, by royal decree
The past tense shall prevail.

At the Statue of Isaac Watts

1
Image set
Among sticky buds:

Dated, the marble
Establishes a prodigal
Home for good.

Clear through traffic,
Trains and horns
The Civic Centre chimes
'O God, our help…'

2
The measured tide
Moves congregations;
Its undertow sways
Outside the walls.

Across the narrow sea
From Western Shore
(Refinery hazy
Under the forest)
An impure land delights.

Against sluggard wit
And muddy spirit,
Dr Watts stands proof.

At his granite base,
Place tributary strands
Of living wrack.

Other

Breakers and wind
Are blinding,
And drown the voice.

Likewise a calm and open sea
Sucks up, casts back,
All images – or else

They are suddenly distant,
Tiny figures just seen, gone
Where the beach curves.

The artist steps through his canvas.

The vociferous I alone
Who made the head ache
With his clapper,
Is an empty bell;

A cave where wind echoes
And dark tongues absorb
The metallic light.

Now the gull's shrilling
Above the wind, or quiet *huk-huk,*
Is a note among many
Belonging to one, one
That is not a voice;

Nor meaningless, unless
Extrinsic meanings

Are found: patterns the wind
Does not draw, webs
Between waves the foam
Does not make.

Monologue of a Shell
for David Annwn

1
Though the sea moves me
Still I wait, wait
For another to enter.

Will it follow
Aspiring snail's long crawl,
Or descend
Through polyp and medusae,
Zones of androgyne,
Down where crab protrudes its eyes,
Jellyfish pulses its bell,
Through dark, torn weed?

Or stay, where
Egg-sac and oiled, salt
Cuttle-bone lie,
Dog whelk comes with its acid,
Atoms thrive between
Irreducible grains?

Will it be
Of these kingdoms
Or another?

I wait as I must
With a patient look

2

Emptiness grows,
Sucking the residue
Of a former possessor;

Expands, draws in
Phantom sun and moon,
Shadow of earth,
Spectre of seas.

How vast
In a tiny space
The ghost of infinity.

Though I cannot bear it
Still I wait.

Without patience
I wait, mouth open
To be filled
And void my emptiness

Birth

I held your mother, child.
She was beyond me.

The shout forced from deep inside
Came shrill: shout
Of a body hurt and labouring
To an end: of a self lost,
Willing unwilled, giving
Delivered.
          I was not afraid
Though a storm's blue light
Flickered on steel, made the room

Tropical, dangerous.
One of the masked attendants,
I held her, beyond myself.

Hair more like seaweed on a stone
Stuck to the crown; then
A creased and slippery form
Came in a gush of blood,
More naked
Than a mussel eased from its shell,
Stranger, more ancient,
Than a creature long-drowned.

Breath came with a cry,
Earthly unearthly cry.
The knot was cut, and tied.

Outside, I watched rain drip
From railings of a balcony,
Form pools on the roof below.

Still on my wrist I feel
The reddish fluid
Where the waters breaking fell.

Gull on a Post

Gull on a post firm
In the tideway – how I desire
The gifts of both!

Desire against the diktat
Of intellect: be single,
You who are neither.

As the useful one
That marks a channel, marks
Degrees of neap and spring;
Apt to bear jetties
Or serve as a mooring;
Common, staked with its like.

Standing ever
Still in one place,
It has a look of permanence.

Riddled with shipworm,
Bored by the gribble,
In a few years it rots.

Desire which tears at the body
Would fly unconstrained
Inland or seaward; settle
At will – but voicing
Always in her cry
Essence of wind and wave,
Bringing to city, moorish
Pool and ploughland,
Reminders of storm and sea.

Those who likened the soul
To a bird, did they ever
Catch the eye of a gull?

Driven to snatch,
Fight for slops in our wake.

Or voice a desolation
Not meant for us,
Not even desolate,
But which we christen.

Folk accustomed to sin,
Violent, significant death,
Who saw even in harbour
Signs terrible and just,
Heard in their cries
Lost souls of the drowned.

Gull stands on a post
In the tideway; I see

No resolution; only
The necessity of flight
Beyond me, firm
Standing only then.

from

ENGLISHMAN'S ROAD

Beidog

Sunlight and shallow water,
rock, stones with red marks
like cuts of a rusty axe,
dark under hazel and alder,
broken white on blackened steps
and below the falls a cold pale green –
how shall I celebrate this,
    always present
under our sleep and thoughts,
where we do not see ourselves
    reflected
or know the language of memory
gathered from its fall?

Beidog running dark
    between us
and our neighbours, down
from Mynydd Bach –
this is the stream I wish to praise
    and the small mountain.

I am not of you, tongue
through whom Taliesin descends the ages
gifted with praise, who know
that praise turns dust to light.
    In my tongue,
of all arts
this is the most difficult.

Soft Days After Snow

Soft days after snow,
    snowdrops
under sycamores beside the stream,
earth brown and crumbling.

Now the dark gleams softly
under catkins and water below,
alight in the February sun.
And I who desired
    eyes washed clean
as melting snow,
radiant at the point of fall,
know that every word obscures
the one I want to know.

Now soft days bear us
who take each other's hands,
and on their surface
    colder than blood
our brief appearances.

Though snowdrops follow the snow,
    and the water burns,
darkness carries them.

Our faces are taken away.

Where do you go,
    unspeakable love?

On Saint David's Day

For Dewi Sant, an eye
of yellow in the daffodils,
the curlew from the sea,
the hare that lollops by a gate
    which opens wide
on far Plynlimmon,
Cader Idris
and the airy rockface
    of the northern sky.

I too would name
a tribute of these things:
cold wind,
white sun of March,
    the boundaries
whose handywork of stone
shines through the falling earth.

I turn towards the mynydd
in a film of light,
    and turning
ask of Dewi Sant
    his benediction
on these words that settle
where the uplands rise.

Curlew

The curve of its cry –
A sculpture
Of the long beak:
A spiral carved from bone.

It is raised
   quickening
From the ground,
Is wound high, and again unwound,
   down
To the stalker nodding
In a marshy field.

It is the welling
Of a cold mineral spring,
Salt form the estuary
Dissolved, sharpening
The fresh vein bubbling on stone.

It is an echo
Repeating an echo
That calls you back.

It looses
Words from dust till the live tongue
Cry: This is mine
Not mine, this life
Welling from springs
Under ground, spiralling,
Up the long flight of bone.

The Mason's Law

Though the slate
where his hand slipped
could not stand
    worthy of a name,
at least it could lie
in his living room.
set in the floor.

Er Cof unfinished,
under our feet, recalls
the mason and his law:
    Honour the dead
with your craft;
waste nothing; leave
no botched memorial.

Brynbeidog

For ten years the sycamores
have turned about us, the Beidog
has run with leaves, and ice and sun.
I have turned the earth, thrown up
blue chip and horseshoe; from near fields
sheep and bullocks have looked in.

We have shared weathers
with the stone house; kept its silence;
listened under winds lifting slates
for a child's cry; all we have
the given space has shaped, pointing
our lights seen far off
as a spark among scattered sparks.
    The mountain above
has been rock to my drifting mind.

Where all is familiar, around us
the country with its language
gives all things other names;
there is darkness on bright days
and on the stillest a wind
that will not let us settle,
but blows the dust from loved
things not possessed or known.

Wind Blew Once

Wind blew once till it seemed
the earth would be skinned from the fields,
the hard roots bared.
   Then it was again
a quiet October,
red berries on grey rock
and blue sky, with a buzzard crying.

I scythed half-moons in long grass,
with nettle-burn stinging my arms,
bringing the blood's rhythm back.
   At night
in our room we lay in an angle
between two streams,
with sounds of water meeting,
   and by day
the roads ran farther,
joined and formed a pattern
at the edge of vast, cloudy hills.

   The house was small
against the mountain; from above
a stone on a steep broad step
of falling fields; but around us
the walls formed a deep channel,

with marks of other lives, holding
its way from worked moorland
to this Autumn with an open sky.

Hill Country Rhythms
for Robert Wells

Sometimes I glimpse a rhythm
I am not part of, and those who are
could never see.
    The hawk I disturb
at his kill, leaving bodiless,
bloody wings spread, curves
away and with a sharp turn
follows the fence; and the fence
lining a rounded bank flies
smoothly down hill, then rises
to wind-bowed trees whose shape
the clouds take on, and the ridge
running under them, where
the sky bears round in a curve.
On the mountainside stands
a square white farm, its roof
a cutting edge, but it too
moves with shadow and cloud.
    I glimpse this
with the hawk in view, lose it
to fenceposts and trees holding
a still day down, and wings
dismembered at my feet, while
down the road comes a neighbour
singing loudly, with his herd
big-uddered, slowly swaying.

As a Thousand Years

Not a soul, only
a stubble field, bales
like megaliths; a flight
of trees over the Beidog,
and behind, darker green,
at the back of the sky,
the ridge damming
the sun; then,
    for a breath,
there was no sign of us.
Not a soul, only
light flooding this field
bright as a marigold.

In a Welsh Primary School
for Mari LLwyd

Around me, elements
of this place form a world,
with dragons, flowers,
flying houses on the walls;
shepherds with real crooks
and kings with tinsel crowns.
Here I also come to learn,
and know the same care
Gwion knows, Aled, Ifor
and the rest; and glimpse
through mist between
two languages,
the kindest things of Wales.

Mari, though I stand outside,
may I be numbered still
with all who give you praise.

Pwyll the Old God

'I would be glad to see a wonder,' said Pwyll
'I will go and sit on the hill.'
The Mabinogion

Pwyll the old god
may look through you,
when you look through eyes
of spiderwebs, through
tiny rainbows brilliant
as bluebottle shards, and see
 in a dance of gold flecks,
the mountain hang by a strand.

This may be his emblem:
a ram's skull with a thread
of silk between its horns,
but certainly you see
the everyday, the wonder:

Old windblown light
fresh as this morning:
rooks with black breasts
and silver backs; clear-cut
shadows brightening fields,
and over the ridge the sun,
curve of a dark body
in blinding white; everywhere
fragments of web shining,
that look like ends.

Emily

The season is late; our long shadow
with two clothes peg heads notched
one above the other lies flat across the field;
and from above me, breaking
the quiet of sleepy baas and caws,
an excited voice exclaims
at a sudden vision:
    a yellow digger
uprooting bushes, changing the stream's
meanders to a straighter course.

Now our single track divides,
a dark fork in dew-grey grass,
and a small girl in a red frock,
sun yellowing her fair hair, runs
away from me with a bunch
of corn marigolds, campion,
harebells and a magpie feather
crushed in her fist.

Away she runs through a drift
of thistledown, seeds
stuck to her bare wet legs;
runs away laughing, shouting
for me to catch her –
but I know now that I never will;
    never, my darling;
but run with care, run lightly
with the light about you,
run to the gate through moist soft grass,
webs and bright blades all about you,
    hint of a rainbow
in the silver shower at your heels.

Lines to a Brother

To Tony Hooker

Waking early today,
I think of you preparing
for work, driving through
a quiet Oxfordshire dawn.
    You will join
sawn timbers, intimate
as their owners will never be
with roof-tree and joist,
while I lie awake, watching
light form the bulk of Mynydd Bach.

    I see your hands,
steadied by the recreation
of labour, and again
the morning air tastes thin;
    once more I turn
to images of the skilled life
we have drawn from and shared,
in whose absence
my words offer no habitation.

Prayer in January

Now when the old New Year
Starts red with sun on snow,
Must resolution splinter
Like a frosted bough?
The stars of ancient January
Hurt the eyes; by day, like stars,
Snow crystals make them ache.
But Yahweh's eyes burn clear
As drops that fall from alders
By the mountain stream.

They are not stars or melting snow
But outstare every star
And every thing most star-like
In this old, cold, flaming universe.

Soft heart, small, bitter pool
Beneath your darkening hemisphere
Of ice, hidden eyes blaze
Where you hide. Regard
Their hard regard, that weighs
The worth of all you guard
At not a fraction of its price.
Let love outlast such love
As self. too tender of itself,
Has dreamed regardless of a sight
More pitiless, more pitiful than you.
Then be unselved, or drying
When the eyes burn through
Die dreamless into hard-ribbed clay.

Sycamore Buds

Then speak, not
from the shell of self,
its beaten walls, but
as these pointed buds
with tight, green scales
the winter could not loose
and waste the rising force
erecting spikes, that
lengthen, curving
into soft, closed beaks
that open on their tongues
and now unfold small hands
wrinkled, blood-red leaves,
fresh and glistening

damp-shapes of the force
they are, containing them.

Dragons in the Snow

Thaw to the hedgerows
left white crosses on the hill;
    the first thrush sang.

Now, a buzzard cries, confirming
    silence under all.

The few bare trees are darker
for the fall that covers
    boundaries,
and in their place reveals
contrasting absolutes.

We are so small,
the boy and I, between
the snowclouds and the snow.

He starts from here,
who talks of dragons
as we walk, the first today
to leave a human sign
beside the marks of sheep and crow.

He warms me
with confiding hand
and fiery talk,
    who also start
upon the ground
of choice, the silence
answering the choice;
happy to be small, and walk,
and hear of dragons in the snow.

from

MASTER OF THE LEAPING FIGURES

Master of the Leaping Figures

Under his hand the great book
glows with lapis lazuli, red,
gold, and in the smoke
of fire-balls falling on the city.

Outside, the torturer's art:
figures hung up by the thumbs,
jerking on a blackened ground.
Devils fill the castles, and the people
reel in a divided land, fleeing
from the horsemen; peasants
are forced from the fields
to drag carts loaded with stone,
and the crops rot.
Men say openly that Christ
and His saints sleep.

Under his hand, they do not sleep.
Here he is master,
illuminating the Word in a little letter,
painting in a tiny space
the beginning and the end.

Lines cut deep in time
meet in his hand: from Rome,
Byzantium, Ireland
and the Viking north;
from tracks hacked through woodland
and seaways marked by wrecks;
from monks of the Saxon minster,
a ruin outside the workshop.

It is not love of violence
that leaps in the figures,
but violent love:

David gripping the lion's jaw;
Moses clubbing the Egyptian,
as a Saxon remembering his home
might dream of smashing the skull
of his conqueror;
Christ thrusting the devil into Hell.

All flame against the dark,
like the prophet who is one
fire with the horses of fire,
blazing against the blue
of a midsummer night-sky
with a rim of gold;
a man barely contained
by the frame holding him
who leaps in flesh of flame
in a world on fire, burning
in the mantle that he passes on.

On a Child's Painting

1
We three play in our garden.

I am the reddest red
and the yellow sun's no bigger, no brighter.
Nor are we smaller or bigger than the tree
which has landed at my feet:
                a green anchor.

I stand looking up with my red eye.
We three are the world:
                the tree
                        the sun
                                and me.

2

Each spider moves enclosed
at the centre of its circle.
The water spins with wheels and shadows
and at the bottom
the sky lies white among branches.

A carving on slate could not be more distinct.
Sunlight through trees
quivers, and its beams on the river bed
bend, and are gold.

But you, small and naked, come
smashing the image to glassy splinters,
with a green leaf stuck to your heel.

For John Riley

Consider also a channel:

image open to the end
leaving no sadness

of mud closed in
a maze of creeks, but

a wind freshening
through banks clear cut

to a river mouth, open
where light streams in

from Itchen Water

At the Source
for Norman Ackroyd

1   The Source

A small pool in undergrowth,
too hidden to mirror the sky,
in which we alone may see
liners plunge in the ocean,
villages and cities
growing on the banks,
or even the small stream
several fields away, gathering
for the course through a history
it does not witness,
though to us standing beside it
nothing seems more like an eye
that sees everything to come.

2   Cheriton Long Barrow

A long low hill in a hill field,
a curve within a curve,
white of ploughed chalk
on pale arable: epitome
of winter's purity and grace,
of lines like the skeleton's
long since at one with its bed
and with nothing opposing it
but the first violet
barely visible in the open hedge.

3   Civil War Battlefield

Over the hill the land opens
deceptively and a mound
covers Hopton's raw men
and Waller's troopers.
The few hedgerow oaks
are motionless, as the storm
of another season builds
slowly in their trunks.
Flints picked up from the fields
look like corpses flung in a heap.

There is no sound but rooks
returning to their rookery
on the battleground,
ewes, and lambs born today
that totter all bloody
to drink their mother's milk.

Tichborne

to Chidiock Tichborne (1558-86),
executed for his part in the Babington Plot

There is no place deeper in earth –
where the young quick river grows
and cressy streams feed it
on beds of purest chalk stones;
and the rhythms of settlement
remember a life before his,
from Vernal Farm through meadow,
copse and ploughland, and St Andrews
standing against curve and swell,
where Catholic and Protestant
share a roof, and members
of his family who succeeded him

figure in stone.
His place is not with those
who gained the world.
Nor can there be an elegy
for one who wrote his own:
the perfect balance
of a man who would soon be
'bowelled alive and seeing'.
About to die, his claim
was a faithful occupation
older than the Normans;
a long life before him here,
which he planted again
on the scaffold, in Tichborne earth.

At Ovington

for Lee Grandjean, sculptor

You would make a form
that contains, which your hand moulds
as we talk, creating a body
between us, in the air. Below
the broad full river glides
hypnotically, silver,
green and dark. Here wind
meets light and water,
and the current at each instant
finds its bed, erupting
over shoals of weed, sliding
through a lucid gravel run,
continually making
and unmaking lines,
as in my mind I catch
and loose its images,
and about our heads
swifts hawking for mayfly

unerringly, explosively, glide.
I would let all go again,
saying – it is perfect without us,
but we meet here, we share
words and your hand shaping
the flow, the brute
and graceful wings.
And our feet beat solidly on the bridge.

The Diver

to William Walker, whose work on the foundations of
Winchester Cathedral from 1906 to 1911 saved the building

1
This was a great cross, shaken,
an ancient decaying tree.
A foundering ship, breaking her back,
Titanic of the watermeadows –
except for him.

He descended each day
to the pitch of death.
Enshrined stillness, turbulence of prayer,
rested on him.

In darkness, with dockyard skill,
he made the foundations sound.

And rose through the graveyard each evening.

2
He rises here still.

He is The Diver:
fish bowl and goggle eyes.
More weird, friendlier, than a mason's monster.

Ropes and pre-war innocence
hang about him.
His globe swims through chaos.
He walks alive among the dead.

He stands here too,
with builders whose face he saved:
a workman offering his hands.

A Child on St Catherine's Hill

Lightly she scoops up
the city in her arms.
Even the winter sky
shares her mood, as it cracks,
scatters silver
over watermeadows,
strikes gold
from the Hampshire hog
of the Castle weathervane.
She sweeps in
footballers running rings
on green squares; racing
boats crawling on the canal;
the Cathedral
at the centre, like a model
centuries of builders
will perfect; all things
that daily enclose us
between the flint
and the red brick walls.
She can reach the downs
far round, the coast, the blue
gasometers of Northam,
and hug it all for a moment,
and lightly let it go.

St Cross

for Jeffrey Wainwright

1

Over the footworn step,
between old walls
that have soaked in
river-damp, in
the twilight nave,
there is something
that is not ourselves.

Something to grasp
if we could name it;
like the tile
with its legend:
>   ***Have mynde***

2

The damp, still dusk
of December breaks,

and light sweeps the aisle
slowly, bringing back
grey sky, grey stone:

>   St Cross

signing the valley
with a man's power
and his penitence,
mindful of
Henry of Winchester,
soldier-bishop,
turning from the world.

3

The light as it passes
reveals an old woman
kneeling at altar rails
of a side chapel.

No ghost, but one
completely given;
as if the body of stone
had formed round her,
and she would be here
after it has gone.

Itchen Navigation

What I love is the fact of it.

A channel kept open, shipping
stone for the cathedral;
blue Cornish slates;
coal from Woodmill
to Blackbridge wharf.

A channel used, disused,
restored, until the last barge
passed under the railway bridge,
now abandoned, framing
water that is going nowhere,
but silts, with passages
the colour of stonedust
and boys rowing, a surface
silver and boiling
where blades dip and turn.

It is the stillness
afterwards, grey water

settling back to the shape
of slow working journeys
during a thousand years.

from Spring Movements

1 May Morning

Misty leafy morning, green and grey,
with a blackbird on a white branch –
as if the image were all
and I their composer.
His call corrects me,
his whimpering notes, repeated,
a message perhaps to fledglings:
Take care Take care Take care
But to me now the sound of fullness.

Cherry blossom in the first spring
returned to Hiroshima.
Here it is on the air and on the ground
and still the branches are pink and white.
All is effortless power,
a giant chestnut lifts a mass of candles.
The eyes of the dead were everywhere

Children cross a bridge above me,
their silhouettes skip and dance,
flat and dark against the light.
From here they might belong to any time,
generation tumbling on the heels of generation

But I am too far away to see,
when I come near they are too real
beginning this misty leafy morning

Crossing the New Bridge

As we crossed the new bridge
you looked through it,
through the view of ships
and oil tanks, and saw
a gravel track, the floating-bridge,
your father with a pony and trap
on the shore. And you said,
'he wouldn't know the place
if he could come back now'.

Later, on the shore, you spoke
of him and your mother,
of being young and in love
and feeling you could walk
on moonlight on the water,
with a man who died long ago;
you spoke, too, of friends
long-dead, and of your brother,
the uncle I never knew.

You looked through near things,
but not into distance.
The man with the trap, the children,
all the people with you,
were real as the shingle and the sun,
and for me the shore
was firm again as it was
at first, when you said,
'they're part of us, we're part of them'.

Inscription for *The Poetry of Horses*

for my mother

I give this
in memory of the shires
of your childhood,
who were ploughed down
in the mud of the Somme,
and left their invisible bulk
heavy in the half-light
of a Hampshire stable
and their brass medals
to furnish saloons
at The Waggon and The Ploughman.

I give this for those
who left you the echo
of hoof-falls, memories
of a playground in their shadow,
of earth that has their shape:
movers of earth,
earth-bearers, slow sure
teachers of patience,
gentleness and strength –
foundations
of your father's house.

Netley: On the Site of the
Royal Victoria Military Hospital
with thanks to Emily

White horses on a full tide,
blue-grey from shore to shore;
blown cloud, blown smoke
over the seaway –

where armies passed through,
and the wounded returned
out of battle.

        If we could see
the mass-grave of memories,
or see with the eyes
of one maimed man,
and smell blood
where the wind freshens,
this place would crush us.

But the space is open wide,
the day restored
to a child's eye, and where
men stared at ceilings
shocked with gunfire,
my daughter sits and writes.

Slowly I spell her words:

the shells that roll under the sea
the waves that roll and swerve
in the sun

from 'A Winchester Mosaic'

Looking up in Nuns Road
I am startled to see

the head of a young man
framed at an upper window
in lamp light, studying,

and in him, in his
intentness, other
figures – scribes, and one
I have long dreamed of,
listening, seeing
with the eyes of the place.

I stand for a moment
watching him,
in a stillness
of dusk-red brick,
the houses statuesque.

At the top of the road,
high in a tree over the stream.
a thrush is singing.

•

Delight wakes in the day
with the daisies, the day's eyes
lifted after frost.

A sycamore, bark flaking
in scales of mossy green and grey,
bares an orange skin.
A fork stuck in a dunghill
wears an old blue bucket
like a hat.

Already the sun is everywhere,
brightest where caught
and broken in a mallard's wake.

The trees of the park
are naked dancers –
not a tremor, only the poise
before the first, slow movement.

*

Twice today it has happened –
cherry blossom scattering
pink and white on the breeze:
walking by the cathedral walls
I have passed a woman
and entered a cloud of perfume
so strong, so sweet
I almost fell
against the odourless cold stone.

*

Old stories
repeat themselves –

the 'oldest resident'
cradled in chalk
at a motorway interchange;
or a man unearths
Roman coins in the cellar
of his Victorian house,
and in his garden
a stone-carved, Saxon head –
Every day
something new.

*

We ripped down
the hands of strangers,
we scraped pain into the walls.

Gradually the house appeared:

　　　　bare boards,
patched and flaking plaster –
broken timber and a small, dusty frog.

For days I scraped mindlessly
till my head ached
refusing to see
what must fill the space.

●

An old man passes slowly.
He is bent over, pushing
an old woman in a wheelchair.

Effort strains his face
but they are talking together
quietly, easily.

　　　　　　*

There is no more bitter taste:

I have seen a devil pictured
in a man's mouth,
the same mouth
that was moist with love.

　　　　　　*

Red brick glows
through the lime trees'
light, cool leaves.
My children run with the dog
chasing swallows.

Dog bark, shout,
echoing strokes
of cathedral bell.

I too once lived here
I shall say.

*

They came with blood and light
in their eyes, where
'The Powers That Be
are ordained of God'.

They broke in the doors.
They entered with drums beating;
behind the troopers
horsemen rode up the aisles.

They hacked at statues.
They smashed the altar
and gashed the Virgin.
They threw down chests,

jumbling bones of bishops
with bones of Saxon kings.
Skulls grinned at them,
level with their feet.

They saw the joke, and took
thigh bones and flung them

against the west window,
shattering the Resurrection.

The blast that scattered
harlot amethyst and rose
let in pure light, and air
their souls could breathe.

*

Shall these bones live?

Shall the living
who die to each other?

*

Jerome, restorer
of broken images,
paints the choir stalls.

 Outside
the world shrinks from highways
and pestilent streets
to the household doors.

A neighbour carrying
comfort to neighbours
may strike them down.

Twilight lays a gold rod
on Jerome's handiwork,
which he leaves,

and goes home, and gathers
his wife and children together
in the inner room.

•

He records facts:

Born in 1899, in Upper Brook Street.
Sailor in the Princess Royal
at the Battle of Jutland.
Cook on the Mauritania.
Window cleaner.

He remembers, when
he and his wife moved in,
cattle were driven to market
up North Walls – now
a defile for through traffic.

He saw an escaped bull
stuck fast in a doorway,
trapping a man behind a table.
'What a mess, there was blood everywhere.'

He recalls the kindness
of an undertaker,
who would visit the dying
with a jug of soup.
'Good for business you see.'

When Upper Brook Street
had a brook, he fell in,
and ruined his only suit,
and missed his brother's wedding.

Since his wife died
he has lived alone
in the same house, in a row
due for demolition.
'There's still love in my life.'

*

Some days I sense
a whole design even
in the meanest shard,
and in dust
a great company
at the edge of sight.

Then at night I stand
at a curtainless window,
with only my face beside
the skeletal moon
of a paper lightshade
hanging in the dark.

*

I make this memorial

for Lucretianus,
who dedicated an altar
of blue sandstone
to the Italian, German,
Gallic and British Mothers;

and for Athelwine,
who founded St Peter
in the Flesh Shambles
in memory of his parents.

Though their works are numbered
among broken things,
time does not waste a gift
that opens the heart.

*

I LOVE JENNY EASTWOOD
someone has chalked
on the church path.

The letters in stone
nearby have weathered
a hundred and fifty years:

IN MEMORY OF
JANE WIFE OF
JOHN SWITZER

Their stones lean together
against the churchyard fence.
She was sixteen when she died.

The message is plain,
and perhaps untrue.
I know nothing
of love's time –

but it is not
the duration of stone
or a shower of rain.

May Jenny love you too,
whoever you are.

*

My mind has slowed
to the rhythm of words.
There is now no more
to be thought or said.

They came as a gift
in the empty house,
unwired, half-decorated,

where I knelt in the light
of a gas fire breathing
dust from the carpet,
wiping dust from the dial
to see the number to ring:

the only strength is love.

from

THEIR SILENCE A LANGUAGE

Steps

First is the feeling,
which I must trust, moving on –
cut into the void.

*

A passage opens –
that is where the drama is –
out of the covert.

*

To attain a truth,
work fearlessly, for ourselves.
We must break our taste.

*

You dance on the edge
of destruction, you dare see
what will come of it.

*

There is work to do
with fire – simplify the self –
charred and blackened form.

*

You finger the edges,
you execute the instant –
gallows-carpenter.

*

A rooted figure,
bound to earth but gesturing
at the open sky.

*

A human forest –
energy between figures,
linking them and us.

*

You shape the image:
it is a bridge we cross over
to meet in the world.

*

To know oneself shaped,
and work with knowledge of death –
that it may bear fruit.

*

Fern, gorse, pine, slow cloud
moving on – 'voice of the rhythm
which has created the world'.

*

One use of space is
for speaking across, another
to deepen silence.

Walking all day in the Forest

Walking all day in the Forest, I saw again how impossible it would be to convey a true impression of the ancient woods of oak and beech without showing that they are movements of light and shadow and air as much as countless tree-shapes; or rather that the natural 'pattern' continually changing around one comes from the interaction of forces and things which together make a world of the most delicate and subtle movements, and strong deep-rooted forms. And this is only to sketch the surface, without regard to the interdependence of growth and decay, or of the many forms of life each with its own world in the world that human senses perceive; as for example insects under a scale of bark, a grey squirrel leaping from tree to tree, a woodpecker crossing a glade.

~

Fallen cliffs, breakwaters

Fallen cliffs, breakwaters – rows of stout posts standing out above the sea – gravel, gorse to the very edge of the cliffs: these things move me strongly.

They belong to love and friendship. Being with J at Hordle gave me the beginnings of a poetry that was really mine. The posts are vaguely human in shape and they stand for a massive effort that is only temporarily effective and has to be renewed over and over again; and at the same time they are completely non-human, insensate, and like a strange thing emerging from the sea. They belong and do not belong, they become part of the sea against which they are a defence, the waters they are meant to break.

A sleeping painter and a sleeping sculptor come awake in my senses there. When I come back the smell of the sea is on my hands.

Black on Gold

He dreams he is a painter standing
at his easel in an ill-lit attic painting
studies in black and gold.
A dead butterfly flutters in a breeze,
dances at the window in a filthy web.
Even when I was a boy (he thinks)
walking with a rod in April among the trees
I tasted filth. How free the mind?
A man – but what (he asks) is a man? –
will do anything not to wake up.
He dreams he is a sculptor hacking
at the block that is himself.
It is black, black as rainwater
from the stump of the tree of knowledge.
Let me let in the gold (he weeps)
but the wood rots under his hand.
He dreams he is a poet writing
a poem about the shadow of a tree
leaning over water, where sunlight
touches the gravel bed with gold.
He is losing his bony grip,
the bank is eroding under him.
Wild bees swarm in the hollow of his skull.
He dreams he is a hunter chasing
the beasts that seek him.
On hands and knees, belly
dragging in mud, icy skin,
he follows where a black stream
runs through bracken into the wood
and a doe steps gracefully to the brink
and bends her neck and drinks.

First Touch

A breath,
a touch of air
that feels so gentle,
so light,
on curve of wing and leaf.

A spider
poised on silk
which binds the furze.

Skaters
making circles,
dimpling the stream.

A fly
borne down
turning and turning.

Touch of the god
with broken hands
who rounds the globe of dew.

'From'

He lifts up his shell
over his back. Does he know
what he is made of?

The shell feels like wings.
He tries to flap them. The wood
grows harder round him.

*

His body holds fast
to the earth. Yet he is, too,
a bow bent to shoot,

and the soul's arrow
drawn back, alive to his touch
in every feather.

*

His body's a bird
made from the bough it sings on.
His wings are the sky.

*

He hangs gracefully
like a hawk preying. Behind
him, poised, his shadow's

a man crucified.
Soon he will stoop and drop down,
blood spit on the earth.

*

Sometimes when earth opens
he grows into her.

He becomes sapwood.
His kin lodge under his ribs.
What is the thing men

boast of? His head shakes:
Man is branded on his brow.

*

He is always that
which he is about to be.
Now as he emerges

from the wood, he is
the tree walking, the passage
that will be his way.

Between earth and sky
his body stretches. He strides out,
and earth underfoot

thrusts and pulls. His flanks
are downland curved on the sky.
He is a flame also –

wildwood flickering,
blazing through trunk and limb,
burning in the mind

of the maker carving
him, consuming dead wood,
shaping him anew.

[*'From'* *is a sculpture by Lee Grandjean*]

Elusive Spirit

What is the quick, and where
is the spirit that eludes you?

There are rumours that seem
to speak of it here:
prickly fruit on a fallen tree –
dark butterfly that whirls up
fast and high, out of sight –

tap tap tap on dead bark,
the yaffle that flies away
crying his ancient laugh.

What stands revealed
for a moment, naked
as nails struck into wood?
All that hardens, dissolves,
dissolves and hardens.

Light stabs through clefts.
Hollows cup dark, in which creatures
that crawled from the sea bottom
millions of years ago
live on decay, enable life.

Even as you look, all
that appears solid transforms
root and branch.
                              Where
with a word you nailed down
that quick and elusive spirit
there is a flicker, a rustle, a sudden
sword dance of one bracken frond.
Dark whirls up with dead leaves
in a gust of sea wind, sun pours
where the trunks stand still.

Lines to M

Crushed bracken fronds, where we lay.
(Remember the nightjar's churr.)

Dry river-bed through the woods,
Torrent of stone, tumbled and stilled.

Oak Song

for Carl Major

Oak
     at the back of the cold

after sedge and rush and Arctic birch
before the thief of fire
before the information of the axe

Noah's oak, laid
in drift gravel
with mammoth tusk

Black rings burnt in the soil

          *

The lover of the tall stag
also appointed concerning the hares
that they should go free

The rich complained
the poor murmured

How sharply the man
in the covert sees
threatened with blinding

          *

Skin for hide
skin for bark
nailed to the bloody tree

          *

Oak
             for the makers of cruck and hull

Pickings of useful parts
knees and elbows
from doddards
though the body be decayed
'Caste acorns and ash keyes
into the straglinge and dispersed bushes:
which will grow up sheltered,
unto such perfection
as shall yelde times to come
good suplie of timber.'

                    *

Saviour, protector, bearer
of the world's wealth –
stripped from the forest
that favourites crawled on,
leaf-rollers, baring the crowns

                    *

Stacked, loaded
at Southampton Docks
for the trenches –
painted by an English Cubist
sharpening his vision.

At Queen's Bower

At Queen's Bower, following the stream through the woods, I saw the heath blue as smoke in the sun.

Water dark green where deep and shaded; ochre, yellow, gold where the sun came through, lighting sand or gravel shallows; a most beautiful transparent green at the point of shelving and darkening. Pulse of reflected water-light on tree trunks, and below, a procession of bubbles, and fragments of foam curling in an eddy, ceaseless corrugation of rapids, infinitely various shapes of branches and sky mirrored in still water, and the currents sinuous as eels. Sun splintered in countless glittering points, or its image held full and gleaming white, like a bright moon.

Returning to the stream from an excursion across an open space, I saw a herd of deer: white rumps and tall antlers moving peacefully between trees, not scenting me, perhaps, yet looking in my direction and apparently at me, without fear, but keeping half-hidden and well out of reach.

There if anywhere it's possible to see only what the Normans would have seen. What would a Saxon feel, even if about his lawful business, when caught up in the woods by a hunting party? Like a hare in hiding, perhaps, when huntsmen and hounds rush past on the heels of a fox.

The Cut of the Light

In hot sunlight
at the edge of the wood
a man's shadow cut
dark and sharp
against the path
beside the shadow
of a bracken frond
fine-boned
on mossed oak roots

Silently the marks that no man can read –
dapple, spot and stripe,
hieroglyphs on trunk and limb –
darken
                or vanish
                                or are suddenly
a multitude of eyes, a blaze

The wood is a net, a wicker
of giant forms silently burning

                Water is the walls
                Water is the canopy
                Water is the floor

Midsummer:
mast and tiny acorns form
berries redden by dark green leaves
silence deepens
                        to the human ear

A multitude of eyes
one blazing pupil

Shadow of a man
Shadow of a bracken frond

Now never now
the season the cycle
bark-year and wheat-year
(we say)
spring wood and summer wood
ring within ring

Beech fountains break
in spray of leaves
Oak walls made of sunlight
stream into the ground

Red King's Dream

Surely it is nothing, like a song
about nothing. Yet it isn't the sun
that dyes the Lammas woods red
as I ride with my men through the trees.

Words echo among the boughs.
'You shall eat of me no more.'
What does it mean?

I hide what I hear with laughter,
with the gift of a bolt to Tirel.
I am the Red King;
I am the Conqueror's son;
my song's the twang of the arrow,
the rough, sweet voice of men.

Why should I fear nothing,
nothing at all, only
the blood-mist of a fading dream?

I was alone in a chapel,
deep in the woods;
it was richly adorned, as befits
a king and the son of a king.
I approved the purple tapestries
embroidered with legends.

They were old, older
than the Forest.
What did they mean?

Even as I looked they vanished;
the chapel was bare,
on the altar a stag,
which changed into a naked man.
'You shall eat of me no more.'

Whatever it means, let it be lost
in the flight of the arrow,
and the flight of the stag,
the great stag,
my beloved who dies for me,
soaking the earth with his blood.

Company

'Mystery amid a great company of tree.'
(Heywood Sumner)

1
The wood is full of wounds:

limbs scattered, trunks
twisted and broken,
shells of sapwood standing
when the heart has gone.

And everywhere new growth
heals the wound, a seedling
needles the leaf-mould,
the dead stump bears a living shoot.

2
The wood is full of voices.

But where, where?
(the cuckoo calls)
where is the word that springs new?

3
Figures emerge from the trees,
stag-headed, wreathed with green leaves.

Darkness covers the site –
which light dissolves, opening
cavernous depth.

A sea wind gusts through the grove.

The space fills with sunlight
and shadows, whispering.
Where, where?
At the centre, the naked man,
wearing the holly crown.

In the trees
forked bodies twist and writhe.
Angels and beasts stare down.

Ghost haunts ghost
among the broken pillars,
under the tattered canopy.
The love song fades in the sigh of leaves.

A god with arms outstretched
bows down to the ground.

4
At the edge of the clearing
the great oaks stand,
massively bossed and knarred.

They do not hug the earth
but possess the sky.
Small oaks grow in their shade.

As we approach, they
seem to look at us –
their silence, a language.

Present

The boy with a fishing rod
follows the river upstream
in April, among the windflowers.

The young man lies hidden
in a net of light and shadow,
naked, with his love.

The father walks under the trees
with his son,
who is laughing on his back.

And we call this *now,*
when the man stands still
in the woods in summer,
on leaves that we say are dead.

Windless Leaf-Fall, with Emily

We smell decay
and the earth-side of mosses.

Puffballs, acorns, mast,
chestnuts, fircones,
leached flints – already
they are half imaginary –

objects for her art class:
colours that will tell a story,
shapes that make a world.

Oak leaves and beech leaves
fall around us,

spiralling down,
creeping through the air.

We find a small, clear pool
of water on a bed
of dead, golden-brown leaves.

And when we are lost
we meet an old man carrying
a full sack on his back
who shows us the way,

downhill, on a path
where we step carefully
over twisted roots;

but I see us dancing –
late brimstones turning
round and round, where
leaf falls lightly on leaf.

The Naked Man
*(With despair, as always
at the beginning)*

1
To begin, to begin again –

      Nothing
could be more dead than this tree.
It was once, they say, an oak,
and once, when the highway
crossed the rutted heath,
a gallows.

Now it stands
naked to winds from the sea,
stripped of the final skin,
bone of the bone.

A broken off trunk
with concrete in open sockets

I think it is like
an ancient being
held together and kept up
by a wooden scaffold.

2
Dead, the riven tree
rears up like a horse
with curving neck leaping
from the bracken –

a silver horse
among the brown ponies
grazing the open forest.

Dark blue clouds approach
threatening storm, gorse
and a few Scots pines stretch far
to the south.

The dead tree bends its silver neck.

3
To begin, to begin again
to make an opening –

What obstructs us but fear?
We must give what we have to give
body and soul.

You see the large, blind eyes.
He is there, the ancient wounded one
imprisoned at the core.

What emerges when you cut down
stands free of you,
and sets you free.

from

OUR LADY OF EUROPE

A New Love Poem
for Mieke

A new earth
where not long ago was sea.

How do the moles know?
Already they snout in pale grey
sandy soil full of shells.

There is a poetry of dykes
against the sky –
a church spire – a windmill.
It is beautiful, and bodes peace.

Clods of earth cling to the flesh
of beets waiting in long mounds.
The unpicked cabbages
have a strangely expectant look.

Someone has lit a fire
in a corner of the day.

Red flames leap;
yellow reeds pierce the air.
But over all grey drifts down,
like silt clouding still water.

This is a poetry I know,
since you give it to me.

In Praise of Windmills

In the north the windmills stand
roundly on land and by water.

I take a leaf from the Windmill Psalter.
I name them, both the little and the great:

Young Hendrick and Four Winds,
Goliath and The Helper.

They have come far, but seem
to have grown where they are,
as native to the Netherlands
as sarsens to Salisbury Plain,
and as worthy of praise.

Yes Quixote was right;
they are monstrous.

                  If windmills
did not exist, Hieronymus
Bosch would have dreamt them.
They are living contraptions,
part insect and part bird;
mechanical creatures pondering
flight; earth bound,
flailing at heaven.

There are windmills in the mind,
alive to every breath of fear.

And things that hold firm:
cross-beams and quarter-bars,
crown-tree and king-post;
windmills that drive
and are driven, turning
indifferent winds to use.

They are labourers
at the brink of water;
old warhorses
that take the starving field.
No wonder people say,
The miller is a mighty man;
his hand spans earth and sky.
The great sails are dancing
but the painter holds them still.

The polder is a blank page
marked with a cross;
                Goliath,
a little windmill but a giant
graced by need and by use,
solitary as a lighthouse
in a sea of blue clay,
in a land raised from the sea.

Over furrow and rhine,
I see the blade of a sail
shining, and think of voyages
and stillness at the heart
of tumbling breakers
where the keel strikes home.

Behind the dyke the wind blasts
and the sea hungers.

Here the windmill stands
roundly by water and on land.

I take a leaf from the Windmill Psalter.
May the grace of the sails breathe in my song.

Noordpolderzijl

1
On one side of the dyke
a long, narrow road points
towards the far horizon.
Herons fish in ditches beside the road.
Ploughed fields flow away inland.

On the other side,
a long, narrow channel
pointing out to sea,
fishing boats moored
between green pastures.
Cows share the last grass with gulls.

2
A sluice, a handful
of red-brick houses –
but the place feels like the end
of a continent, somewhere
to sail from, over the rim.

What is it like to stay:
to live with the distances,
to lie down and wake at the level
of tides, listening, feeling
the pressures of the sea?

For generations, one family
has kept the sluice.

What keeps them, perhaps,
is *polderlust:*
a deep, slow rhythm
that ebbs and flows,
changing the sea to land,
and the land to sea,

and sometimes a quickness –
skim of the first swallow,
oystercatchers abandoning
the mud for the sky, piping,
dancing their mating dance
over the edge of the world.

In the Market

I wake from a dream of death as falling endlessly through darkness.

Later, in the market, we stream along slowly with the crowd.

A girl chats to a customer while her fingers expertly fill and tie a bag.

Her skill gives me pleasure.

Men in white overalls shave slices off round, yellow cheeses
and hand them to us to taste.

How shapely the fruit and vegetables, how firmly they fill out their skins.

Gradually I reinhabit my body.

Among all the fish with sightless eyes, the eels, in yellow plastic crates,
are still alive.

They move their bodies against each other slowly, coiling and uncoiling.

I imagine a terrible gasping.

Something deep inside me, dull-flickering, dreams of breathing in the
depths of the sea.

Westerbork

To the memory of Etty Hillesum

1

Our path lies along the Milky Way
and from planet to planet –

then out from the trees
and past the grey saucers
of the radio telescope.

Among toadstools, under oaks
loaded with acorns, we find
a solitary, white earth-star.

2

A few late foxgloves on a bank –
'sheltered'
I say, and the word echoes oddly.

Who can resist the ironies?
When will we recognise
that irony is not enough?

3

How understand the faces, Etty?
You looked at them
from behind a window
and were terrified.

You sank to your knees speaking
the words that reign over life
and bind you to these men
in the depths:

'And God made man after His likeness.'

Did you know they would murder you
and your kind?
That they would drive even children
into hiding, and hunt them down.
And the patients. And the doctors.
All would be sent out on the Tuesday morning train.

4
The black train, which an artist
in the camp painted, looming.

But what amazes more
is his painting of a typical farm
and farmyard beyond the wire
as he saw them,
as we see them still.

5
At first there is little to show –
a few irregularities in the ground
of what might be a park.

Then we see what we expect:
a wooden guard-post,
preserved, or perhaps restored.

Below it, a short stretch
of the railway track reaches
from buffers towards the east;
broken off, twisted, the rusted iron
curves into the air.

6
And there, incised in stone,
a verse from Lamentations.

*They hunt our steps, that
we cannot go in our squares…*

You were a fountain of life.
Your love flowed into the world.

You looked for meaning
and found it in the worst,
accepting 'all as one mighty whole'.

But the faces – how shall we accept
that you could see in them
instruments of destiny?

Whose faces, Etty?
What are they like?

7
Back from the universe,
back from the world,
back from the streets
of Amsterdam,
back from the houses,
back from the rooms
and the rooms behind the rooms,
you were driven, and driven in.

The space of your freedom
was at last a book, in which you wrote,
passionate to understand;

a mind behind the white face;
a card, thrown from the train window:
'we have left the camp singing.'

Reigersbos

Up in the wind, we hear a noise
of stick knocking on stick, a retching,
and looking up see long beaks,
long black hairs like antennae,
hunched figures, cloaked in grey feathers.

No longer the familiars
of ditch or dyke,
or bird flying east, flying west.
No more the hunter stick-still
at the lip of a rhine,
or the ancient one – pterodactyl
rising suddenly in evening light,
or statuesque on a rusting barge
moored under city walls.

Not now fishers
of common margins,
but strangers, rocking
on rafts of branches and twigs.

High in the wind, on tree crowns
echoing rounded, bright-edged cloud,
they clack their beaks
and look down at us with yellow eyes.

And what are we who gaze back,
wanderers over the brink of our own world
who have stumbled into theirs.

In Drenthe

for Rutger Kopland

1
A May morning
when oak buds prick into leaf
and the peewits tumble and cry.
Downriver, faintly, the cuckoo.

It is not what we expect
when a greenshank flying down
from a fence post lifts its wings
to reveal white feathers, and is
for that moment, an angel.

And surely the only one in this country
where the river flows rippling,
pulsing, and the sun kindles
the powdery sand, and beats
with white fire in the water.

It is more than we expect
and more and again more, when
the woods open on a meadow
yellow with dandelions
and you say, simply, 'It is a gift'.

2
Autumn, and the greeny, dark
river carries grass and leaves,
flowing slowly,
serpentine through meadows.

The glaciers crawled so far
and left the granite boulders
and the sandy ridge, the Dogsback.

And here the megaliths came
with the Neolithic track –
empty tombs, dark-gleaming.

In the blue sky, a daylight moon.
In the woods, toadstools –
red-capped, yellow, grey.
Stinkhorn, erect with shining skin
or half-eaten by flies.

So much to see, so much
to taste and touch.
But also a spirit that eludes –
in the light just so
on red leaf and yellow leaf
spinning, turning slowly,
as though each chooses to fall.

Island Cemetery

Within sound of the surf,
lapped in the sand of Grey Monk Island,
lie the dead of two wars and many nations.
From white headstones,
each at an angle, looking up,
the named and the nameless speak:

A. Wilson/Wireless op./Air Gunner/Age 18.
Master J.O. Roberts/S.S. *Firth Fisher*.
Sergeant Borret and Walter Weizel.
Ein Deutscher Soldat.
Inconnu. Mort Pour La France.
A Soldier of the Great War.
Known Unto God.

How tidily their graves are kept,
sheltered in a hollow among dunes,

each plot filled with cockle shells,
sea-washed, white and blue,
under the sign of the cross.

How orderly the lines,
how clean the words that speak to us
of the dead.
It is right to honour them.

We are stilled, hearing only
a faint bee-hum and the wash of the sea.
A salt air mingles with resin from Scots Pines
and a scent of roses.

Then we hear the birds –
oystercatchers, curlews, gulls –
all the different voices.
Shelduck fly over, long necks outstretched.
A harrier scours marsh beyond the dunes.

This is their world, and was
in the beginning – the same and again the same,
where they pipe and shrill and cry
whether monks keep the hours
or bunkers are built on the sand
and the dead wash ashore or drop from the sky,
mangled and burnt.

The sand does not quake; blood
does not cry out from the ground.
Only now we are not at ease
with a peace we have not won,
imagining an earth cleansed
of hatred of nations,
with a beauty that deceives the living
and simplifies the dead.

Rotterdam: Zadkine's *De Verwoeste Stad*

1
Bronze Atlas, with a mortal wound.

But still powerful:
a contorted giant, hands raised,
reeling in agony. Not defeated.

He is the city that will live again
when a bird builds its nest in the place
of his burnt-out heart.

2
When he was a boy
our friend saw the sculpture
lying in pieces, waiting
to be assembled and raised.

Now he often leaves his office
during the day, and walks on the waterfront
watching the ships.

He thinks of his father and grandfather,
of the river that will go on
when he is dead,
and he feels glad to be
'a minor part of it, but a part'.

Does he know how much rests upon him?

How lightly he shoulders this world.

Dreaming of Europe

How good our nights and days
of making love on the roof garden
among spires and towers
lifted up on a level with clock faces
we did not see

*

THIS COULD BE A PLACE OF HISTORICAL IMPORTANCE

He has a taste for ambiguity
which he inscribes in stone paving
in front of the cathedral:

1. Something happened here you should know about.
Do not spit or dance on the spot.
Cover your head.

2. It is just possible that something important might happen here.

3. Think about it.
You could change the world.

*

It is certain that when she was a little girl
the big black thing frightened her.

Now we are overawed,
the blackened stone spires
look down on us.

Inside, the upsurge of power,
graceful, light.

It is invested with a presence:
the after image of bomb damage.

How many did it save?

*

It is impossible to leave the parapets of Europe.
You cannot abandon the fathers,
they come after you with retorts and muskets,
scissors and rolls of cloth.

You may trek across deserts
or sail over the rim of the world,
but the germ is in you.

            Even in dreams
columns of water thunder to the ground,
cities are swept away.

Or a white wolf sits in a walnut tree
outside the window, looking in.

*

We learn to walk with the Christ child
on a walking-frame.

With a windmill, he teaches us to play.

He opens his arms with the generosity
of a drunkard.

Magnified in the minds of men
he becomes a demon who drinks our blood.

*

I believe in Hans Arp and Sophie Taeuber
and the visitation of angels.

Angels are no economists.
Magnificently
they squander the light.

*

Does the wood see, does the field?

It is not after all the worst thought
that no one watches, spying
into every shell-hole and crack.

*

Longing is the road they travel.

Every one a stranger
searching for the lost home.

It is not here, not there.

*

After they were driven out
they sought shelter in a cave
and wore garments which they wove
from animal skins.

It was the best time, they would learn to say.

On a Portrait of Edith Södergran as a Child

Nothing can stop it happening, Princess,
for already with your wondering
and frightened eyes you have chosen –
flash of gunfire over the frontier,
black flags at the sanatorium window:
a conscious dying – into life
that is shaped anew?
No one will prevent you, child,
from flying to the rooftops,
alone and eaglehearted – to look out,
to pluck the strings of a lyre
that stretch from roots of forest trees
to stars that take their fire
from the furnace burning in you –
pale and deep-sea creature,
magic child, woman whom no one knows.
Nothing will abort the birth
of a man-god, poet, or stifle song
within you, which you feed with blood.

Verdun

in memory of Franz Marc

Thistles, poppies, blue cranesbill
by a dusty road.
In front, under the cloud stack
of an August sky,
                        the chalk ridge.

Trees, flowers, the earth
all showed me every year
more and more of their deformity.

                        *

On a bluff a machine-gun post,
an iron mask with two eye-holes,
looks down on new growth.

Inside, the remains of a gun,
rusted and twisted.

The mask that blinded
has survived the face. It overlooks
slopes with harebells and young pines.

In spiritual matters new ideas
kill better than steel.

                        *

Deer feel the world as deer,
but whose landscape is this?

All things, all creatures
are on fire. *All being*

is flaming suffering.

Under pine needles, the earth
that bled for purity
is matter,
                pulped and shattered.

I dream of a new Europe

         *

EN MÉMOIRE DE FLEURY DEVANT DOUAMONT
She is our lady of Europe,
her chapel stands on rubble
under pines, on blasted,
cratered ground.

Where the village was
the woods are dark and still
but the chapel in a glade
is filled with sunlight.

A white butterfly wanders in
and flutters outside the porch.

         *

New Year 1916. *The world
is richer by the bloodiest war
of its many-thousand-year history.*

And all for nothing.

[*The words in italics quote, or adapt, translations of Franz Marc's words.*]

Towards Arras

From Picardy and the land of the Somme
the late summer sky had lowered,
become a roof of dark blue cloud.
And it broke in downpour, shattering
on roadside memorials and regiments of graves,
smoking across the fields,
the mounds and ditches, that already,
after seventy years, look prehistoric.
As we drove towards Arras,
slowly, against the pounding
and blinding cloudburst,
I thought of Edward Thomas
and how he would have loved
the violence of this passing storm.

Hieratic Head of Ezra Pound

Scholars will speak of vision,
even, without irony, 'the final vision'.

The mind of Europe
founders among its ruins.

Words must fail.

The man looks up. The light of the stockade
glares in his eyes.
He is guarded, and displayed.

There is no shadow for him here,
unless it is memory
peopled with shades:

Gaudier
in his studio under the railway arch,
a man of the renaissance,
the air between them alive with ideas.
They dispose of an age of statues,
a trash of books.
The poet is quick to give.
The sculptor works on the marble,
winning every inch
'at the point of the chisel'.

Naturally, the sculpture
will survive the carver,
and outlast the model.
It will gaze back down the century,
over the work of other men of order
whose material is flesh and blood and bone.

The head looks impassively over the ruins.
The poet looks out
towards the mountains, beyond the Pisan cage.

The Mother of Laussel

You may know her by the rock
she is made of, and the scars
of the ice.

She is the one who nurtured the bison,
and starved it,
and holds aloft its horn,
which is also her symbol,
the crescent moon.

She is without a face.
Is she, then, Goddess of Love?

Examine the deep breasts,
the bulging thighs,
the curve of her belly.
With her free hand
she points down, between her legs.

She stands at the cave-mouth
and is herself the cave.
This is the birthplace
of the rock rose and the sabre-tooth.

You will recognise her
by a touch, when, for the last time,
you kiss the cold brow-bone
of the woman who bore you.

Bethlehem

Over all, suddenly, with a crash
that sends sheep scrabbling
at stone walls or squirming in the dust,
a jet fighter crosses the target area.

Over David's fields and the trunks
of felled olive trees, two thousand
years of life compacted, swirling
in the wood. Over stony fields,
hard, white hills and Herod's
mountain tomb crowning the wilderness.

All look up blindly –
women from weeping at Rachel's Tomb,
soldiers at roof-top gunposts,
Arabs selling fruit in Manger Square
or at lathes turning out holy figures,
a tourist enjoying the ironies,
who remembers another place:

starlight on the home fields,
voices drawing closer from door to door
O little town.

*

They will sing a new song
descending from the fields
of galactic dust,
from the black cold
by the blaze of nuclear suns.

They will come down
out of the nebulous dark
to the ruined stable,
gas shell and shattered atom
lighting the night they blindly stare at

*

And so we enter
under an old doorway
made to keep out animals,
and descend through histories:

between pillars stained brown
as old canvases, under
ikons and a brass hanging lamp
balancing a tsar's crown,
past symbols, past stonework
of Crusaders, Armenians, Greeks.

Under the gaze of Elijah
over the long falls of his beard
we come to the mosaic floor
and the floor below the floors,
down to the simple place

all has been built to protect,
or bury...

when, suddenly, with a crash
that shakes the walls,
a jet fighter crosses the hills

and we stand with candles
shaking in our hands

                    *

Lantern light on faces
under the shadowy cross-beams.

So the scene is set:

Mary wrapped in a night-sky cloak.
Ox and ass, big-eyed, nuzzling
into the cradle.
Joseph leans head on hand, resigned
to what he loves but does not understand.

                    *

A smouldering warmth,
fire in the dead of the year,
a red glow at the heart
of black cold, and starlight
falling through the broken roof,
a smell of hay,

the child's cry among the farthest stars

Walking to Capernaum

1
Such violence struck here –
a new thing, a word with power:

And thou, Capernaum,
which art exalted unto heaven,
shalt be brought down to hell.

A gentler word
where the sea laps the shore:
the damsel is not dead, but sleepeth.

2
What I feel most is the heat,
and sick at the unreality
of bad art:

a sloppy English poem
which someone has fixed on a wall
at the site of the miracle
of loaves and fishes;

new stained glass daubing
the interior of the chapel built
over the rock where Christ
is said to have said to Peter…

Compared to these,
I could love the wooden donkeys
and camels and holy families
from the factory at Bethlehem.

Unreal, in a sweat of heat
and bad blood, I dip
my seamy face in the water.

It tastes of salt, and is
a dull silvery blue
on a day of desert cloud.

A crane – not, thank God,
a symbol – but a white crane,
with long, wispy hairs at the back
of its neck, stands
fishing in the shallows.
A black lizard looks at me
over the edge of a black stone.

3
On the road between
orchards and tomato fields;
in the dust thrown up
by tourist coaches;
between columns
and among pine needles lying
on the ruins of Peter's house,
I try to imagine them:

The girl waking surprised
with hunger in her eyes;
the woman cured by a touch;
that loud cry, the man
on the floor of the synagogue –
torn and empty, but clean.

What had he seen? What thing
had cried with his voice?

And the fishermen
as they put out –
from this moment, no
denial will swerve their aim.

The port they left behind
is a heap of blackened stone.

4
It is evening, and very still;
heavy cloud, the colour
of smouldering ash,
obscures a misshapen moon.
Tiny fish swarm blackly
on the surface, nudging
crusts from our seafront café.

Suddenly, the wind rises. Trees
sway and open, lights go out
and napkins soar into the air;
waiters leap to catch bottles
and glasses blown off the tables.
A cloud swirls through the streets
and covers our plates with sand.
At once the sea heaves up
a huge, slippery shoulder
against the wall.

In the sudden violence
I see them for the first time;
the small port waiting, still
waiting – nets spread on the wall,
barrels of salt fish on the quay –
and the men who will not return,
but are borne up at a word
as their ship drives through the storm.

Homer Dictating
for Gerard Casey

It is the body that speaks
and what it speaks of is the man
and his suffering, his thought,
the vision he sees in his blindness.

His hands speak,
and his mouth speaks more than words,
and his whole body,
an old man's but still powerful.

In the depths behind his eyes
warriors boast on the windy field,
Odysseus adventures on the seas,
among magical and dangerous islands,
and strains his eyes against the light
and sting of spray to catch a wisp of smoke
far off, rising from the hearth-fires of Ithaca.

Rembrandt's Homer is a man,
but the light of the sacred
is upon him –
a pale watery gold
falling across his shoulders and his face.
But it does not shine from afar,
from another world.
The sacred is part of him,
dwelling in light and shadow,
and his body is the landscape of his soul.

For the painter has taken clay in his hands,
common clay,
and shaped from it the image, God-given,
which he knew in his own world,
among merchants and soldiers,

Rabbis and adventurers,
the grand and the poor of Leiden
and Amsterdam, and knew
most intimately in his own flesh,
in the imagination that is breath and blood and spirit.

With this he saw, and humbled his seeing
to know the vision of the blind,
of Homer dictating,
with sightless eyes,
the seer of men and women and gods.

from Europa

for Lindsay and Phoebe Clare Clarke

The sun stands naked
out of the shade, in a space
of poppies and fig-trees,
                          an empty space
where Greeks and Romans built their worlds.

                    Over all
the breath of the bull-god,
the sear of lightning that burned
a blackness into the light.

What havoc it caused –
columns, sarcophagi,
a headless female statue,
the dome of St Titus,
                    emptied,
filled with flutterings
of sparrows.
              And a side chapel
where the faithful and the sick
bring medicine bottles,

prayers for healing,
ikons of the Virgin;
where I placed a bunch of grass
in memory of a dead poet, a woman
who knew the value of such things.

*

Once, they say,
Earth was a giant pithos
pouring out oil and wine
embracing the dead.
                            No war troubled
the forests and mountains
or bloodied the inshore water.

Then the air darkened
with the flight of the god.
She clung unwillingly to his back,
fingers wound tight among the curls,
that moments before had plucked flowers
where she walked by the shore.

And so, with the waves
still swimming in her eyes,
she was laid down and the bull
hung over her, a cloudy mass,
                    and bore her down.

It was here, under the plane tree,
where the stream runs
and the water is living,
                    never so living,
under the naked sun.

from 'Earth Song Cycle'

Women dancing in a field of poppies

Slowly at first they measure
their steps as the sun strengthens,
the poppies flame redder,
the sea-blue deepens, and they,
women in white, loose-limbed,
flowing, circle hand in hand,
turn faster, and faster,
leap and fly till their feet
are birds, white birds, skimming.
And round they go, wing to wing,
as the field revolves and the sea,
and earth veils and unveils,
white and blue, under their heels,
which skim and pause and come to rest
while round and round them turns
the scarlet field,
                              and O the earth.

And every cleft is mute

A cry echoes among the mountains.

                              Somewhere
the earth has opened. Where?
Where is her daughter?

She searches and searches
but finds no sign.

Who cares? Not the god
who leaps and dives and plunges
to death in ecstasy
and forms again among the foam.

Not the stones she kicks over,
or the cuttle-bones
or globs of tar.

Not the roots she finds
sodden with salt –
                    images
that would bewitch her,
grotesques
with human form.

Are these, maybe, a sign?
She calls again
and no one answers.

The sea changes.
It is clouded glass,
into which she looks, and sees
nothing.

No one. Every cleft
is closed against her call.
She sets her bleeding feet
on shells, weed, foam.

Turning over, the waves
are cavernous,
smooth for an instant
and full of sand.
                    Light rides in
on crest and underlip.

The day will be immaculate,
the night perfect, that sees
her torch wandering in blackness
like a moon.

She hides her golden hair

Let him bellow,
                     the thunderer
wrapped in cloud,
for this, she says,
is only the beginning.

          Birds
returning to her without a message
drop dead from the sky,
snail shells bleach in heaps
spiralling down to dust,
snake and green lizard
crawl into holes to die.

And she hides her hair
in a hood.
                    As a stormcloud
falls on the harvest,
blackness blots out the gold.

               She walks alone
among her people, searching
their sightless eyes
for a sign.
                    No one answers
when she calls and calls.

Men break picks on the fields,
oxen strain to shift the plough,
seeds fall on soil turned to stone.

               She will waste all
as she is wasted,
calling and calling.

Ovens and storage bins,
the giant pithoi
that poured out the bounty,
all their round bellies
hold emptiness and mould.

And this, she says,
is only the beginning.

        Afterwards
the fall of ash,
sea white with corpses,
no swellings on earth
but the bloated dead.

        Let him look down
on his handiwork,
              thunderer,
father of desolation.

        Who will survive
to make an offering
or give him thanks,
when she, who brings
all things in their seasons,
provides nothing,
and no one but the dead?

Written in clay

What could he do, the swineherd
gaping at the meadow?
            Had he dreamed
the earth had opened, closed,
his herd gone squealing down
along with her,
        the fairest flower?

174

What could he do but wait,
and learn, maybe, that flowers spring
from rotting flesh.

*

She will come back (they said),
the sweet, red seed is on her tongue,
she will return
and we will taste her words.

       And when she rose,
she will descend (they said)
she will descend again,
and rise
     there is no end,
spring air returns,
the birds repeat their calls,
the wind of winter wails
in trees and round the house
the same old song

    no end

       no end

He looked (the squeal
still ringing in his ears)
and everything
       everywhere
spoke to him of her

She was the water and the fish,
the stream within the stream
becoming flesh,
she was the black grain and the bread,
the wet clay and the pot,

the light, the dark,
the silence and the word,
she was all formless
on the verge of form, and form
becoming formlessness.

And so he tasted on his tongue
the song
and sang it to a lute
made from his flesh and bone

and wrote it in the clay

    no end

      no end

That Trees Are Men Walking

A poem dedicated to David Jones

Dry-mouthed, in a dry time,
the polluted summer air grey,
I sit down to write a poem
I have been contemplating
for twenty years – an elegy.

And find nothing,
nothing to say
about death. For
the man who died is alive,
his images flow
in the channel that he made.

Yet there is a story to tell.

It begins with a bear,
a bear that the boy sees
in a London street,
a muzzled bear,
held on a chain,
a bear which he draws, dancing.

It is a story about a bear,
and about a boy who becomes a soldier.

A bear in a London street.
A soldier caught in a tangle
of barbed wire, torn khaki
exposing his private parts,
a human being in a place
that he shares with rats,
mules, shattered trees,
dead men,
trees that are men walking.

                    *

The artist mixes his saliva
with the pigment,
and spits on the cave wall.

It is not himself he paints,
but the living creatures.
But he is there, at one
with the herds that flow across the wall.

No doubt of it, no doubt at all –
he makes himself at home.
There he is, too, a figure
moving across the heavens –
the bear, and the hunter of the bear.

                    *

A ruffled air.
A closing among trees,
the crucked branches fallen still.
Who was sitting there in his place?
(He was a child, but that was ages ago,
before the spit dried on the rockface.)

Whose scratch marks?
Whose pawprints?

Was it Artio, mother
of the Bear who rules the Honey Isle?

Trust him to recall the names,
more than the names,
this man of courage
who descends into the hades of oblivion,
who will leave none to perish.

Does Artio wake in the cave,
or is her body the cave
from which we issue,
emerging to read the scratch marks,
follow the pawprints,
going with care over the forest floor,
penetrating the tangle,
learning to dance?

                    *

Grandfather Bear

            who gave his bones to the altar
            his flesh to feed the tribe
            his skin to clothe the being
            who shifts his shape,

                becomes the bear
                who dances

Mother Bear

                who digs under the roots,
                makes herself a bed,
                licks her paws, sleeps.
                When she emerges, it is spring;
                her cubs blink about her.
                She licks them into shape.

Brother Bear

                in a London street,
                brown bear on a chain,
                which the boy draws – dancing.

                    *

At Capel, in love
with the shape of things:

Dai, in his army greatcoat,
framed in a window, engraving.
Or walking with his friend
to unblock the stream
and free the waters.

Rhythm echoes rhythm
for the hunter of forms –
hill-shapes, trees,
hart's-tongue fern,
the horses that return
without riders –
the men betrayed to death.

Falling waters loose,
bind and loose,
shaping the ways of change.
And mist – mist crumbles rock.
Cloud packs hunt the hills.

Clouds, and mist, and something
that is neither,
a story of change woven
around the things that change.

That the dead men lie down
in the shattered wood,
shed their skins like snakes,
crawl back to the womb that bore them.

*

I paused by Nant Honddu,
by the dingle where David had a cell.
It was an enchanted place,
but what I saw was no dream.

The waters are dying, the trees
are being torn form the ground,
silt builds up in the rivers of the world,
the Thames, where he floated
the ark of his imagination,
the Rhine, the Danube
and the effluent of Europe,
the Brahmaputra,
the Nile, the Ganges,
the Euphrates, where Eden
is a desert of smoking wells.
We are making another earth;
the creatures we drew from the rock
are going back, fading,
their rhythm a distant beat.

Before the figures of the dance turn to stone,
before there is no voice left
to tell the story of the serpent
coiled around the mountains,
the serpent of drought
that Indra slew, freeing the waters,
before there is no hand to draw the bear,
no one to tell the wonder tale
of the bear waking in the cave,

      pray for us, Dafydd.
      David the Waterman,

      pray for us.

from

ADAMAH

from 'Seven Songs'

City Walking (2)
for Sarah Hemming and Julian May

Today I imagine her walking,
seven months pregnant, resting
from the effort of working with her husband,
in their terraced house in Old Woolwich Road,
preparing a room for the baby.

Down narrow brick lanes she wanders,
past iron bollards, like cannons stood on end,
behind her the Royal Observatory on the hill,
across the river, on the Isle of Dogs,
Canary Wharf gleaming, dominating the sky.
And here are the gantries, industrial chimneys,
almshouses, immaculate in the shadow
of a power station with dirt-white, peeling walls.

Through a gate at Highbridge Drawlock,
down a slipway, onto a shore of shingle
and sand, where she stoops, fingering
shards of pottery and brick,
glass jewels, among the stones.

         Low waves flop over,
swirl round a rowing boat swinging on a rope.
Sunlight glitters in millions of eyes.

     It is peaceful here, the city
is a distant rumble; traffic,
railway, power station, refinery,
corn mill, voices – all one sound.

I let my mind move with hers over the water,
past seaweedy, green walls and piles,

converted wharves, leisure complexes,
docks, offices to let, stone church spires,
past woodwork, ironwork, ladders
descending into the water.

Today she is in love
with the city and the river,
joining and dividing, flowing through.
Silently she recites the names of bridges:
Tower Bridge London Bridge Southwark
Blackfriars Waterloo,
                              her mind drifting
until she sees a heron on the deck of a rusting barge
and the sight fixes her.

Sunlight in millions of eyes
glittering on the surface, through which she sees
the water's body, and feels
the channelled weight, the wild
and voiceless mother tongue.

I would follow if I could, out of sight
of fixed and finished things, power
and after-images of power;
out of the city fractured
and constructed – the city
that is not one, but shaped to millions of needs.

For a moment only I think she enters
the place where no one can dwell,
the dark tide that generates,
pushing into gaps and inlets, carrying
driftwood, silt,

and emerges, rested, strolling home

Before the day set hard

In sleep, I cried –

I was a story that was being told,
a fugitive that fled with bleeding legs
and felt a hot breath on my neck
and on my back the thwack of staves.

I ran and ran but could not move.
My body was a beaten bush,
in which I hid, a tiny bird.

And woke. Or seemed to wake,
sleep's waters parting as I felt for ground.

And now I walked in fields above the sea,
a place of furze and granite tombs,
each Cyclops-cave an eye of dark.

And there I saw the Sun in Majesty,
which melted as I watched,
a molten rain that fell in gold drops on the sea,
and cloud that mushroomed into space,
and turbulence of cloud,
a chalice spilling poisons on the earth.

Where I looked west,
the salt fields of the deep
were Lyonesse, and palaces
of tangled wrack, and leaping rocks
were dolphins turned to stone,
or submerged effigies of ancient knights.
And overall a wounded tanker
wallowed, bleeding oil.

I walked upon the cliffs
and heard a small bird sing,
a jingle and a trill which rose and fell,
a strident churr.

Don't ask or seek to know, a voice said then.
The story being told is what you are.

I trod the waters of a dream,
and reached for ground, and heard
the strange voice say:
You are a woman at the door of time.
Imagine, then, anew.

Then in a dark-mouthed tomb,
a Cyclops-eye, I saw an eye,
a tiny, bright and living thing.
I saw a cocked-tail flit,
and sensed, so near, a clutch
of breast-warm eggs which nestled
in a globe of moss and down.
So near, before the day set hard –
         but must it set?

Or shall I tell the story as I choose,
and walk on cliffs above the main,
and see the sparks of furze, and feel with her,
the hunted bird that dwells in caves,
the bird who makes her nest inside the tomb?

Cyane

Finally a body that is water's own.

So at times words seem to come to me,
as though I could speak,
or as I remember speaking in another life.

I pool to a glassy stillness.
I move slowly, mirroring
shapes & colours of leaves;
housefronts, walls; a face;
the world entranced
gazing at the world.

Or quick, a stream
of silver – only
what I know is imageless,
except once, in another life…

My moods are stagnant,
turbulent. I circle circle circle,
or stand motionless, or pour out,
falling, scattering,
coming together with the smoothness
of a dolphin's back, an icy glide.

What was I before I was finally this?
Sometimes I dream that on my surface
I form a human face,
and look out at another,
red and glistening, a man's,
and arms, in which he grasps a woman,
binds her to him, drags her down.

And it shakes then: earth quakes,
and springs apart – they are gone.

And I shake, the being that I was –
                    skin blood bones
unbinding, flying into drops,
flowing with a constant tremor,
plunging down, shattering,

shaking out long and smooth,
always broken, always whole.

And over I go and over,
and under, and round and round.

But what is that but a dream
that I was human once,
who am pure spirit,
not bodied, nor bodiless,
but water in water, quick
with a life beyond all words.

Silence, then; or a voice
that is the sound of water running,
in which, if they listen,
any one may hear a tale
of terror at the roots of things:

a tale that I tremble to tell,
half remembering, or inventing,
but as if, once, it were my own.

Groundless she walks

Her footstep strikes
the dusty track.
               Heat-haze
on ripening wheat creates
a shimmer in which the gorged pigeon
flaps away losing shape.
In dark places, in their own spheres,
minute creatures webbed in moisture
vibrate at her burdened tread.
And she feels down through cracked earth,
knowing something about them, sensing
the rhythms by which they live.
And what, she thinks, are their constellations,
what gods burn in their heavens?

Do they too know a Cassiopeia who holds up her arms?
Are they companioned, or unsupported
except by physical law,
sheer materiality, lumpen as flints
which will indifferently turn my ankle
or break a plough?
                    Instability
was the mark of the day when she woke.
She has been at the edge
since first light crazed mirror and window glass,
froze the lightning of the garden tree
against the toppling tidal wave of earth.
She is a woman carrying a child who flinches
at the momentary thought she is a man
who dreams herself to be a woman,
and who now is walking beside a harvest field,
kicking up the dust,
                    alone, afraid.

What is possible? she insists, feeling
again the movement under her heart.
                    Who was it said
'the march of time'?
Months weeks days hours minutes seconds
hard boots striking sparks from flint
regiments tramping from the cave-mouth
                    down the years.
And must it be so, faces
with the same blind look ever
appearing, disappearing – one likeness
dominant as Jupiter in the night-sky?

An obstruction in the flow: blackness
shot through with flashes of light,
scintillations,
her mind itself the sky
in which a woman lifts up her hands

over heavy-headed wheat,
the whole sea of the field whispering.

But she may not dissolve;
she must absorb turbulence;
the desire within to be other
is the pressure she must bear.

But must the story repeat itself,
the flame be kindled to burn as one
with the whole fire that consumes and dies?
Let me take a seed of thought
and find for it a cryptic niche,
some damp place under soil or under bark,
a home of bacteria, of creatures
that live in water, and grow there
a being that moves to another rhythm…

But now her mind is an ice-berg
in a polar sea, mountainous dark
moving under her, bearing her along.

And instantly the image fractures,
and dissolves.

What, then, is possible? she cries
silently, as groundless her footstep
strikes the dusty track.

The child I carry
will crawl into the world.
What ground will he stand on?
What humus, or piece of debris
hurtling from the supernova,
the giant star that once was man?

from Debris: A Cycle of Poems

From debris
of collapsing stars,
from gas and dust,
where nothing is wasted,
a stream of images.

Ground-ivy

Hobnailed
imprinting the soil,
Adamah stops,
bound to the spot,
wondering at the tiny
smoke-blue flower
that bears his mother's name.

Night Piece

Cut of farm roofs, black
against sunset,

owl hoot sounding
the depths of woods:

the present is a blade
you could try with your thumb.

It is a haunting thought
that there are no ghosts,

only this black and shining edge.

Owl Country

Where the beck trails
alders and dark
feather-headed reeds,
at the foot of a post,
a pellet:
compacted fur,
yellow teeth
with which a vole
would gnaw
           no more.

Lark Song

Springing
from clod and flint

rising
invisible

or a black dot
quivering

raining over
and all around

song shower
in April air.

Angels at Salle

I feel for them:
                    spirits
bodied in stone, motionless
winged beings the wind abrades,

soldiers standing at their post
on a long-abandoned field.

Palimpsest

Hand-painted,
the stories of death
and resurrection;
in the margin,
matters of business,
manorial accounts:
fodder, grain, sheep.
Requiem, eternam…
et lux perpetua.
Here, too, in the light
of workaday transactions
the poetry of meaning.

Magnolia

Flowers opening,
foxglove-red at base,
creamy shell-like petals

scatter your images on the ground
where the tree springs,
flowers erect,

where it moves in you
and the only word
you feel in your mouth
is **tongue.**

For Quickness

Observation (looking at the magnolia) can become an idol.

Why should seeing be painful, unless one is possessive, wanting to see all?

It is feeling with, feeling into, that respects the other.

Distance makes this possible. There is no other way of coming close.

Pastoral

A field gate,
five bars of weathered oak,
goose grass cleaving to them,

a gate stuck open
permanently,
rusted chain hanging.

Once the way
from the fields to the horse pond
in its semi-circle of ash-trees;
from the pond
to woods solid with shadow,
through woods to the church,
stone wildmen and dragons,
to labourers' homes.

You may say it opens on
a world that is dead.
I would reply that,
like the goose grass,
this is where I like to be.

Not Newton

The old bramley
bowed down
under the weight
of big apples

a red admiral
feeding on
a windfall

a green woodpecker
flying away
laughing

nothing
but
energy.

Hare

Fear of us makes
the heart jump,
the body leap, the long legs
run uphill, and stand –

Absolute hare,
long ears laid back,
long skull, our image
a gleam in dark eyes.

Blackberrying: A Conversation Piece

Whether birds feel joy in their flight
Whether one's lifework might be something no one wants

Whether one will end up living in a cardboard box
Whether love is an element like air or fire
Such are the questions on their purple tongues.

Hogweed

Skeletal
on a hedgebank
against darkening sky

you imagine it
a wizard's wand
to conjure up the wind and snow

a telescope
to focus on
the Christmas star

a pipe
in fingers
stiff as ice
to play the New Year in.

Reading Walls

A late summer evening
darkens, light rain begins
to fall, swallows wheel
over us where we peer
at walls webbed with age
and feel with our fingers
signatures, initials,
names hand-cut in brick,
rough lines of those
who made the track

through the fields, dug clay
from the pit, wielded
the rusted scythe
that hangs on the barn wall
under the swallows' nests.

Earthling

How many space craft
have left for far destinations,

planetary, heavenly,
ideas carrying their cargoes

of visionary beings
who will not return.

Far-seeing, or new-born dead
in your shrouds,

I am your fellow,
strange as you are,

but let me stay, smelling
earth and pond water at dusk.

Walking to Sleep
A poem for my mother

Hours before you died,
I read you once more the poem
you first read to me
in which the merman mourns
for his human wife

who has left the sea
and will not come away,
down, down, who will not come away.

Then you, whose life
had been to care and comfort,
were walking to sleep –
                              walking,
counting the stones the shells
dog whelk cuttle-bone
shepherd's crown
fairy loaves anything
of interest on the shore
in sight of the Island
in sound of the sea.

Walking, walking down
where, hours before,
you heard a voice that said
'Start again, Start again'.

                    *

This is the shore
on which you loved to walk
in childhood, as a woman
with a family, and in age.

                              Walking
in love and in sorrow,
not looking away, but finding
in yourself the place
where you were most alone.

Walking, and always finding
something of interest –
driftwood, pulse of sunlight

in water, gull floating
on the swell.

What I think of now
is that place,
and of you watching, listening,
as I cast your ashes on the sea.

                    *

Your father was the same,
wanting no stone to mark his life.

Was it humility, or pride?
I only know he lived in you,
as you live in me.

Here are countless stones
and on all and every one
the print of memory…

What can I say that is not untrue?

You gave me love of poetry,
and with it, knowledge
that words are a shore
on which one must walk to the end,
and look far out, hoping
to glimpse the thing, the being
that one loves, and must let be.

                    *

Ash and specks of bone,
which a breeze blows back,
making a grey smear
on dry shingle,
which the next wave covers.

Yes, the tide is coming in,
the next wave leaps farther
up the shore, sluices
the shingle as it slides.

Beyond the swash,
the tinkling, shifting stones,
a gull dives down
out of the bright, late sun
and settles on the sea – one gull that seems
to have the whole bay to float on.

*

The martins we often watched
have left again,
their holes in the cliff-face
look down where sand falls,
clay slips,
and a notice informs us
that this is an unstable place.

For you, on this bright day,
winter almost here,
no place.

Spots and patches of light
dance as the waves break.
White light,
greeny-grey water,
ash that is blown back
and waves fetch and cover.

Now, for the first time,
you who would gladly comfort,
look away.

*

What is the scent on the salt air?
I search, and find
a few late flowers:
sweet alyssum,
tiny white faces
among rocks, sea defences
of Portland stone.

Shall I lend you my senses
to know once more the finds
that every day delighted you
and bound you to the world?

I do not find you in this ash
that vanishes among the foam –
ash that is less than anything
you lingered over,
                                    walking
counting pebbles shells
bladder wrack dulse
kelp with a holdfast stone.

It is not words that hold you
any more than shingle keeps
the water that sluices it,
sifts, running down,
changing its shape.

It is not you who dissolve
as I come to the edge of the shore.

from 'A Poem for My Father'

Oak branches tufted with grass
mark the winter floods. On banks,
between leafless trees, yellow
of primroses, first daffodils.

In the stillness,
a woodpecker's hammer-notes vibrating.
From a wooden bridge, I scatter ash
which the current gathers,
bears down
moving in snaking lines,
smudging dark water,
reflections of branches and sky.

                    *

I follow the way of the water with my mind
            flowing –
through wood and meadow,
under Boldre Bridge,
past the Shallows, where he painted
and I fished with my first bamboo,
the quick mirror-surface distorting us,
as here, it twists the trees.
            And for a time
all seems colourless,
until I look close and see again
the darkest dark that is depth
of colour – sky-and-water mix
of yellow and blue and brownish green,
the surface bark, or a nest of snakes
shedding their skins,
flicker-tongued adders of fire
dissolving in depth, the bodied
escaping appearances,

the bodiless the broken the whole
 flowing through.

*

It is the knowledge that dies,
stories one half-remembers
without the voice,
no particle of the living
reducible to an image or a word.

 In this region
there are no appearances,
no painted surfaces, only fire
that burns with the life in things.

To hold it
is like putting your fingers in a flame,
or trying to bring back an object
from a dream –
treading down firmly on the stairs of water,
rising slowly to the air.
And at last something clutches
at your wrist and you wake scared,
hand tingling, your empty, open hand.

Not like Icarus
for my brother David

Not like Icarus – your white legs,
your strong, man's legs,
out of the water, up in the air, waving.
And I looking on from the shore
as you stood on your hands on the sea-bed –
astonished, longing to follow.

How powerful you seemed,
how indestructible,
your crawl into the waves
a total mastery,
your disappearance
a certain prelude to return,
hands dripping with treasure.

But water was not the element you loved.

I remember the silhouettes
on your bedroom wall, the diagrams,
the balsa-wood models –
Lancaster, Heinkel, Hurricane –
all the exotic names and shapes,
as strange to me as flint axes
and mammoth bones, but to you
the romance of the real, freedom
you would learn to master.

I don't believe in your death,
you are too much part of the world
that held you, free of the air,
as I once saw you when I was a boy
and you were a young man, diving
for a handful of gravel and mud,
waving to us with your legs, surfacing.

But words were not the poetry you wanted.

I remember the excitement
with which you ran from the house
at the noise of low-flying jets,
the look of a boy on your man's face
at the far-off sound of a speck
that seemed to float in the blue.

Nothing could compare with the drone
of the engine, ground spreading out,
cloud streaming past and the sun above,
your surge into the wide, blue sky.

Then you would dip again, down
to the earth that kept you
for a time but did not hold you.

Hardy of Wessex
to Donald Davie

We go back to him,
thinking we can read his face,
like the land's –
Mr Hardy's, writer,
late of Max Gate, Dorchester.

What we want him to be, he is:
our elegist, whose heart lies
in the mould that shaped it –
from which we conjure him,
melancholy as a robin in winter
whistling on a tomb.

He is our shade, but
it is we who haunt him, walking
the dungy by-ways, shadowing
the cloud-dark Dorset heights.

Still he looks down at us,
on the road he too struggled up,
scattered with the shards of our armies,
lit by the glare of nuclear fires.
We look back, reading in his face
the stories we tell ourselves,
that are not true.

For a Woman Who Said
She Could Fall in Love with a Boat

For Mieke on her fiftieth birthday

What I wish you is not a sieve
or a chugging tub
or a hulk half sunk in the mud
with ribs that clutch at the sky,
but a sound bottom,
good timbers throughout
and oceans ahead to plunge in.

Or a canoe, maybe, or a kayak,
for mountain lakes and rivers,
skin or bark rider of rapids
and a wise spirit to guide you –
sickle-gleam glimpsed between cedars,
new moon drifter on dark water
                    bringing peace.
Or a rowboat,
oars dripping,
crawling in creeks – where you anchor,
and lie back, head pillowed,
and dream, rocking, rocking,
watching the sailing sky.

Or else a thoroughbred yacht,
sail taut as a fin or billowing,
gull-white hull with lines
sleek as a great northern diver –
a yacht which never dives, but cuts through waves
over the crab's den and the lobster's lair,
over stones and mud where the weeds are,
under, down under, while it races over
and ocean is its pasture.

Better for you a boat like a dolphin,
a mythical craft,
part mammal and part bird.
Nose up, nose down, and the back curves
out of the water, awash and shining.
What are you then but the sea
and the sea's daughter,
waves riding waves
and spume in your hair?

Best of all though I wish you
one of your native boats.
Not a *tjalk* with a hold
full of vegetables and household stuff,
or the floating barn of a flat-bottomed *aak,*
smelling of grain and stone to mend roads.
No grandfather barge which you would care for
like a beloved elder, retired
from the work of the world.

Rather an antique sailing boat
with brass portholes and polished timbers,
stately and playful and worthy
of every weather,
canal-wise and ocean-knowing,
a boat with an engine that never fails,
and room below when you carry a fellow voyager,
and a red sail.

from

ARNOLDS WOOD

'Hopeful young trees,' we said,
as we planted them,
colleagues and friends,
digging down through the matted grass.

It was a day in February.
White blossom against black sticks
in hedges, frogspawn in the farm pond.

From your home field
on the Cotswold ridge,
we could see the white horse
on the edge of Salisbury Plain.

The wind was cold, and felt like snow.

*

Do we abandon the dead
by leaving places where they died?

Ask the daffodils
by the Haycombe road.

Ask the fields
of Newton Park, the stones
of the castle tower.

How should one be
here
who is nowhere?

And by what right
do I ask?

As though I could command
any spirit, or a dead man

had less right than the living
to be left alone.

*

Sometimes
it is as though things
themselves want to speak:

ancient walls, buildings,
the bridge over the Avon,
autumn ploughland,
pasture on the Cotswold ridge.
Almost, in the air and light,
         a voice.

Or perhaps it is a feeling,
even a dampness
which earth and stones exude,
and we may interpret,
calling it continuity.

But what time is it ever
for the living except the moment?

And for the dead,
this is not their place.
They are not like the stones
that speak of them.

They are not here.

*

Sometimes in this country
cloud conspires with stone
to make a prison for the spirit.

                    The man
I want to talk to is alive
in the detail of his poems.
It seems that, reading.
I could call him out, ask
whether what I am making
is a place he could inhabit.

Help me, I want to ask,
to avoid the humourless
self-importance
of middle age.

                    *

Wool caught on a thorn
tells a winter's tale
to the empty fields.

He is beside himself
transforming the stage
to a world of sheepwalks
and golden fleece.
Sheepman and wife
lying together in effigy
quiver alive.

He is telling again
the tale of things we met with
dying and new born.

                    *

Poet, teacher:
did it drain you
to quicken the life
in other minds?

Below me, a mallard
dives and rises, dives
and rises,
stands up in the water
shaking
in ecstasy.

*

Old stonework,
monster faces with open mouths,
for seven hundred years
the same expression
gaping & leering.

Did I think you too
belonged to the long centuries?

*

Outside,
clear evening light,
a kestrel hovering
over the young trees
we planted in your memory.

At table, it is almost
as if you neglect us.

*

Smoke from burning stubble
hangs in the air
over hill fields
towards the crematorium.

Impossible to think
of oneself as absent,
all one's roots
entangled
in the world.

*

One thing you can be sure of:
death will change our lives.

*

The year comes round
with a shiver.

It is the time when,
sitting at your desk,
I found among your papers
the poem of home-making
you had written for me,
and which I read then
for the first time.

Green light at my window,
rain dripping from leaves,
cold spring rain
shivering.

*

The trees are still small,
but high enough to hide
all but the stone wall
canopied with ivy,
the roof and the walls
of the farm.

Cloud over chalk ridge,
a man full of life
pulling a cork
pouring in our glasses
red wine.

*

The black car
that tore into silence
left a distant hum.

The world has closed
behind it, leaving
the faintest breath.

I start out to follow
plodding
on my two feet.

*

It is just possible
you will teach me
to make a friend of death.

from

SCATTERED LIGHT

Brother Worm

1
One moment in Valdivia
when the ground under him rocked
he learnt that land also is a sea.

One moment is enough:
no security can hold.
From high to low,
all that is immutable shifts.

Along the coast, in Quiriquina,
at Concepcion, it was as though
a fleet had been wrecked – timbers
that were roofs, furniture, smashed,
strewn on the beach, storehouses
burst open, merchandise scattered,
rocks, even rocks, torn from the deep.

Far from home
the ground moving from under him
like the *Beagle* in a cross ripple,
or more like ice, thin ice, that bends
under the body's weight.
How describe the sense of it, the world
that stood for all that was solid,
in a moment, gone…
                            as an earthworm
through its skin knows vibrations
of mole's snout, or bird above,
beak striking down

2
He has read the runes –
nothing magical, only

the commonest unnoticed
evidence – castings,
half-decayed leaves
dragged down, inches
of black mould
accumulating.
               At night
on the lawn at Down,
he has gone with a lantern,
seeking to know
with vibrations and light
the mould-maker.
Indoors, on the piano,
he has worms in a pot
of earth, and plays to them.
Also with a bassoon,
and whistle. And with his breath
which they feel only
when he breathes hard.
Blind, deaf creatures,
how alive they are,
how sensitive,
sifting the soil, burying
and inadvertently
preserving monolith,
atrium, tessellated aisle,
accumulating over
millions of years mould
that bears crops, as he
in a lifetime gathers
facts. Pertinacious man,
who recognises under his feet
a fellow voyager, another
with presence of mind,
adapted to the world
it moves in.
Such are the powers

beneath notice, one
observed that steadies
the observer, makes possible
also the unsteady world
in which he moves,
breathing through the skin.

Liefje

A scrap of life, but,
awake, she fills the room –
ears back owlishly, paws
off the ground, dancing
on her tail, or flying
through the air sideways.

Asleep in a corner,
the house curls around her
with a mind of its own

dreaming of cat.

With a cat on my shoulder

Forgive me, Liefje,
this isn't about you.
It was the feel of your fur
against my neck that brought back
my mother's words: 'he loved cats,
my grandfather, always
had a cat on his shoulder.'
And there he was, an old man
I had never seen before,
feeling with pleasure
a cat asleep against his neck.

Homage to Ernest Zobole

for Ceri Thomas

1 BLACK VALLEY

He stands in the doorway.

He looks round corners.

He reads lights and stars.

He belongs as much as a dog
nosing in corners.

He is a stranger.

Sensation was his teacher.
Knowledge on fingertips.
A taste on the tongue –

Black rain,
soot-fall light.

Black that reaches into everything.
Black that is a fount of colour.

2 IN AND OUT OF THE FRAME

He was everywhere and nowhere –
earthbound and aerial,
prisoner and free man,
man and ghost.

Look and you can imagine him flying,
or see him stretched out, a corpse in the street.

He stands in the doorway
mixing fact with dream.

Forget views – the painting
is the place, the painter
is the place that made him.

3   NOCTURNE

Blue was the space he moved in

Blue was what the jackdaws saw
what the dogs sniffed in terrace corners

Blue the bruised and wounded flesh
the seams and masked faces

Blue the unseen

Blue the sea and the freighted ships
Blue the night-sky where the little yellow stars were

Blue the river and the shadowed valley
Blue the windows with a splash of yellow

Blue the taste of the Welsh rain

Blue was the journey that had taken him a lifetime

Mosaics 2

THE MASTER OF THE ACTAEON MOSAIC

Imagine him arranging the pieces,
assembling the design, fingers
growing a skin that is strange to him.
His days too are pieces now,
each a jagged tessera,
which he places, fits, designing
a picture that tells the story
of a young man who entered a place
forbidden to men,
and paid for his trespass.

Quickly death came to him,
he thinks, but not quick enough:
torn by his own hounds, shredded
by slavering jaws.

Imagine: piece by piece
he assembles him, the youth
with hair grown to fur, skin
the flesh of a stag, hands
and feet hooves, that speed
over the ground – too slow
for the dogs – his dogs –
his named dogs, that do not hear,
but fasten their teeth in his neck,
his sides, and tear him

      piece by piece

which he forms, assembles,
as days come and go, each
a jagged tessera, a fragment
of the same story, as he works

in the cursed land, fingers
growing to skin that is strange to him,
far from the field of Mars
and healing power of the Roman sun.

Like thistledown

As a word surprises you
sprung from the language net
drifting across the mind

you don't know where it came from
you don't know what will come of it

but there it is, floating down
or, though you felt no breeze
flying up rapidly
                    out of sight

a winged seed
with connections whose beginning and end
you can only guess at

which may catch on a bird's wing
or land where in time
it will lift a paving-stone

or, like a word no one receives,
drop in a web, like a spider,

        a dead spider.

To a woman with a sunflower

Here are two faces
side by side, one smiling
for the warmth that fills both.

Dearest, no one draws you down
to the cruel and narrow place
that was your childhood once.

It is not I alone who call you back.
It is these faces shining
full with the light of the sun.

Self-portrait with falling leaves

1
After long stillness
a breath
which the wind-chimes felt

Night music
and a rattling house.

2
Dawn in a shower of colour,
wind ragging the nest of the woods.

What I love though
are the countless differences
words point to, but cannot catch:

a boat rocking on air
an arrow gliding
wings that turn or float or drift
this slow one downing that would love to climb
the other quick as a bird:

a leaf, and another leaf

each itself, but all it seems
one – a fall
that lays open the heart of the wood

this circular flight which seems
for a moment
endless.

Not the new poetry

A blackbird pecking
an apple left hanging
on the tree – a red apple
with a white cap of snow.

It's like nothing in the world
but another blackbird
landing on another branch
which quivers, shedding
a little snow.

Owls calling on a winter night

which to the listener
sleepless in his bed
sounds like 'Where, where?'
and an answering 'Here, here'.

But who knows, who knows,
silence returning
with a fever of human fears

Snow like thought

because it arrives
seemingly from nowhere
small flakes wandering
sideways
down & up & down

then faster, heavier
bringing up
deeper silence
from some place not dreamed of
that was always there.

Butterfly cloud

After days without a breath
still and hot
the white buddleia stirs,
wings open, whirr, tremble,
and cloud –
Atlantic cloud – moves
with a sea of fresh air
into opening sky

Butterfly extravaganza

Hairstreak of light, speckle
under orchard trees…
something's taking shape,
outside, within.
        Then the day begins
to turn, spinning,
scattering light –
red   pearl   brimstone   green –

a blur, illegible.
You catch at words, you say:
admiral – fritillary – tortoiseshell
but each is a hook that will not hold.
          Suddenly
there are eyes everywhere,
and the sun's power pulsing
in millions of veins.
Afterwards the air is still,
restless. Do not trust a leaf.
You fall asleep, and dream,
or maybe wake, seeing
the perfected form:
a purple emperor sailing
high over oaks, escaping.
Opening your eyes, you catch
the day emerging, unfolding
broad, blue wings.

The Bramley at Moor Farm

Old trunk,
iron-rooted, bowed
how delicate the shadow
of your leaves upon the grass.

Winter variations

1
This is the hazel nut
the squirrel did not want:

an empty house
charcoaled with decay

the devil's granary
the evil eye

2
The scarecrow skull
sits grinning on its pole,

the north wind blows,
the rag-coat pockets fill with snow.

Orphic fragments

Song journeys
from mouth to mouth

tundra to tundra
on foot, with horse & mule & ox

over water, by log boat & sail
from coasts of China & Japan

north to the Arctic
south to the Pacific

crossing borders
light to dark to light

words mixed
with saliva & blood

one song journeying
in countless tongues

*

Eurydice
very Eurydice
gone

        *

The world I left to seek her
was the world she kindled,
fire that is the very life in things

Her voice pierced me
and echoed everywhere.

And she is only a feather
a curl of dust?

I will not say what I saw was only a phantom.
Can I say I lost in turning more than a dream?

        *

Out of this world there is another nature
no one can speak of.

Over the border the dark
is not night nor the shadow mist.

You cannot say 'tree' or 'flower'.
No word conjures substance or shape.

Tell me then, what is the use of poetry?

I could answer: poetry gives the rowers
the rhythm of the stroke
and when the sea roars, soothes it,
charms the rocks and lulls the dragon to sleep.

This I can brag of, but what I desired most
no word could deliver.

And so I sing.
And my words fill with emptiness.
And longing becomes my song.

Friend with a sunburst

For Jim Insole on his seventieth birthday

Call it a shield, a boss, an image
of the wheeling sun. Call it
what you will, but I say
this is miracle also.

How it shines!

In fact, something of earth,
where water and fire have met,
and mind and heart, quick
in the hand moulding the clay,
letting the image form,
mastering the flaming sun.

I'm amazed at the burst of it:
creation contained in an image –
an old story
new as the first time told, colours
fresh with the maker's kiss.

Call it also a gift that rings
with his song – a world
played into being, hand and heart
and voice at one.

How it flames but does not burn.

How it bursts but does not break.

Call this also a gift for friendship's sake:
a form that kindles, and sustains –
a shield, a boss, an image of the wheeling sun.

* *Jim Insole's sunbursts are embossed and decorated ceramic plaques*
  embodying the artist's religious vision.

from 'God's Houses'

St Faith's Little Witchingham

Ground elder, nettles, red campion
a semi-circle of lime trees,
island among Norfolk fields.

Inside, we step into emptiness
a familiar musty smell
sunlit white walls. Here though
how dramatic the fragments of story –

a man's leg twisted violently
as he braces himself to deliver the scourge,
a ladder, placed as it might be
against a house wall, to bring down the body from the cross.
Thomas feels with his fingers for the wound.

Such violent action
drawn with delicacy
and gentleness, so that, almost,
we can see the hand moving with the brush
scrolling vine leaves,
rounding a grape, touching in
the forked, red beard.

Nothing is missing
though so much has gone.

Only plague finished the work
leaving life in this empty decommissioned shell.
Soon grass will be at the windows,
leaf shadows move with the vines,
ground elder, nettles, red campion
rise up to bury the nameless stones.

Inside, a quick hand brushes the walls.

Cathedral

'The greatest error of historical Christianity is linked with the fatally limiting idea that the revelation is finished, and that nothing more is to be expected, that the building of the Church is completed and the roof laid on it.'

Nikolai Berdyaev

1

True: we can see
what must happen.

As the raft of logs rotted
on which the stone ark was built,
so this too will founder,
and return, past
the mason's marks,
to some jumble of stone.

All pomp, all history,
all lies and half-truths,
both boasts and gentle memorials,
marks of the meek, signs
of the mighty,
every kept bone,

each pinch of dust,
all of it, gone.

So we may imagine,
who won't be here to see.

And wind picking over
crumbled earth
and some jumble of stone
as wind picks over
the Giant's Ring on Salisbury Plain.

2

But this is different,
you could say.

We know the story;
it won't be lost.

Images,
electronic images,
will probably remain.

How should that matter
to a heart that hungers,
to a creature
with a passion for prayer?

What survives, then,
but a sense of incompletion?

And a people who are poets
at the core – who expect.

They will stand wondering
in this place, feeling
wind picking over
ground where the building stood,
dissolved like cloud.

They will come with questions
they seek to answer.

Questions that are themselves.

St Bartholomew's, Winchester
In memory of Elizabeth Bewick

Most of this place lies underground –
Old Minster, New Minster,
Hyde Abbey, dissolved.

Site then of a bridewell, where
prisoners labouring with mattock and spade
threw up bones, broke open
a coffin, sold the lead –
as men will, who need to live.

We, too, met over broken things,
a marriage, a beloved friend
whom you'd cared for, dead.
In your cottage by the church
we talked, discussed poems, shared our grief.

They are digging there now,
near the plot where your ashes lie,
finding, perhaps, a bone of Alfred
or his son, but digging, always digging.

There were books here a thousand years ago,
a Bible, a *Liber Vitae* picturing
a monk holding an open book
inscribed with names of a company
copied by God in heavenly pages.

You loved the old building
where you worshipped, close
to your home, the grassy plot
with a few trees, a thrush singing.

Yours too was a book of life.
You were a love poet in old age,
a poet in sickness and in health,
even in hospital, when you nearly died.

Only death would stop you seeking
the words, the rhythm,
the exact emotional shape.

And now your ashes have joined
the detritus of centuries,
where everything is history,
archaeology, digging, digging,
reading fragments of bone.

It is a place littered
with broken things,
but you are no part of these.

On the stone path,
pausing among the tombs,
I hear your words, and feel your spirit,
which is never still.

St Mark's Pennington

1
It was the churchyard where gorse ends
dug from the Common,
our playground,
once known as Donkey Town –
not in our time, though
cattle and ponies strayed in
from the Forest, and, yes,
now and then a donkey or two.

Neighbours lie there now.

In old age, the rows
of white stones horrified my father,
though by then he could see them
only in his mind.

2
At Evensong the bells
called me down, past the gorse
and grazing cattle, past
the pond that was usually dry.

I loved especially the words
'troublous life' on the parson's lips.

'O Lord, support us all the day long.'

3
What little devils we were,
snorting in our hymn books
at suspicion of a fart,
turning *pilgrim* to *grimpil*…

But it was there solemnity claimed me.

Shining brass plaques with heroic names.
Language rolling among the pews

like sea in a cave, and above all
my father singing,
his voice raised above all the rest.

Boldre Church Revisited

My father and his cousin
painted this church,
companionable artists,
easels among the tombs,
each with his vision
of aged brick and stone,
red against grey,
the tower on the hill,
New Forest woods below.

He gave the painting to the school
which I attended, close by,
where I began to know myself
a little: a fond, foolish boy.

One Christmas, stiff
with fright, I read a lesson,
my Hampshire burr carrying over.

Older, the Hood Chapel
drew me in, imagining
lives torn apart, walls shaken,
the peace of this quiet place
exposed; as, of course, it was not.

Reminiscence tempts –
a recital of decomposed memory

sprouting half-truths,
ways of the little self,
a bubble of identity,
the whole river
that powers on, forgotten.

It was a day in spring,
the first drowsy bumblebee
humming past, daffodils
and primroses on the banks,
when we scattered my father's ashes
on the river below. I saw briefly
a whitish smear sinking
in opaque depths as the current
bore them down and away.
Above ancient oaks
with the first hint of leaf,
the church stood out,
red against grey.

There was nowhere
I could think of he would rather be.

St Issui, Patrishow

Into the Black Mountains,
raised to the sky,

buzzard cry, kronk
of a raven below

narrowing lane toiling up, past
Nant Mair and holy well

past the stone where Giraldus
came with Bishop Baldwin

preaching the Third Crusade
into the small church

with beautiful carved oak
rood loft and screen –

what's this, or should I say who!
Mr Death I presume,

hands full with hour glass
and scythe, a spade

hung from his arm.
Not today, mister.

From the porch, stone
floor splashed with dung

see mountains and sky,
in a mud nest overhead

swallows, little faces
looking out, eager to fly.

St Peter and St Paul, Mappowder
With thoughts of T.F. Powys

1
Muck on country lanes,
good dirt,
and fields of Blackmoor Vale
and distant Bulbarrow.

A place where a man
might hide himself from the world.

This, however, was a man
on no map known to us
though he chose to live here,
close to the churchyard wall
communing with the dead.

His tomb is a stone book,
the last enigmatic page
given over to the grass.

2
Obliteration
was his word for death,
a final consignment
of all he was to silence,
a gift to God's Acre.

There is, perhaps, a mystery of the self
that reaches beyond the self,
a silence that deepens
beyond the word.

3
I have sat where he sat
in a pew of the empty church
listening, wondering
about this man.

I have followed his steps
on the Dorset lane,
smelling the good smell
of sun-warmed dirt,
watching skylark and peewit
over fields towards Bulbarrow,
entranced by tiny things,
grass seed and celandine,
ditches humming with summer.

I have read his words
and thought at times
I glimpsed a mind I might know.

But each time he escaped
as perhaps he too, listening
for the dead beyond the wall
escaped from himself, reaching
into depths he could not fathom.

Salisbury Cathedral : The Bust of Richard Jefferies

'I look at the sunshine and feel that there is no contracted order:
there is divine chaos, and, in it, limitless hope and possibilities.'
                                        Richard Jefferies

1
What is this man –

sad-eyed, with a beard
birds could nest in
if it weren't marble?

They brought him in
out of the wild,
refashioned him:
a Victorian worthy,
with a niche in the habitat
of bishops, burghers, and knights –

this man who disliked churches,
who found spires poking up
from cornland and downs
an offence,
who wished ruin on temples.

2
Would he seek refuge here today?

On Liddington Hill
he would hear the M4
and smell the fumes.
At Coate Water, estates move in.

Or say Wild England lives
where he knew it, in ditch
and field corner, where
I have seen it with his eyes?

3
If there has to be a statue
let it be one a bird can shit on,
something one can imagine
feeling the wind –

as I felt the wind blowing
through his words,
breaking images,
leaving knowledge
a heap of ruins, driving me
back from the known.

4
There are words
that scatter dead languages,
words that break
statues and statutes
that hide what is real.

This man walked out
of the life prepared for him,
smashed the marble forms.

He opened himself to chaos.
He lived by the quickest word.

It will not be petrified
by this absurdity.

Listen to the wind rising
among the monuments,

preparing to scatter them
like pieces of eggshell and leaves.

Kilpeck

1
Allt-yr-Haul,
Hatterall Hill,
this 'wooded slope of the sun'.

Border country
where names are exchanged

where nature springs from human loins
and all is creative flux.

2
All praise to the master
with strength and delicacy in his hands
imagination at the tips of sense

knower of man and woman
falcon and deer, fish dog and boar

God's creatures, his inventions
all wrought in the web
figures of high art,
sculpted

dreaming magical dreams
monsters
beast tongues
bursting buds.

3
Falcon and deer, fish dog and boar
creatures of the chase,
quarry of lords

who harried this land,
masterful men
who grasped creation in their hands.

4
All praise to the maker
of sculpted forms,

of woman as the mouth of hell,
ravening cunt,
mother of the myriad forms.

5
And who were his masters
if not masterful men

lords of the chase,
castle builders, drivers

of men and women
who slaved in these fields,

who lay down at last
with falcon and deer

with oxen in the red soil,
flesh blood and bone

builders of the border
under Allt-yr-Haul,

Hatterall Hill,
this 'wooded slope of the sun'.

Eglwys Hywyn Sant, Aberdaron

'astronaut / on impossible journeys / to the far side of the self'
R. S. Thomas, 'The New Mariner'

A saint without a story –
we may imagine him,
Saint Hywyn,
in the stone church beside
the stone beach, watching
seas break on the sacred island,
committing his prayers
to the airways and the waters,
faithful to the evidence
of things not seen.

A man we do not know
A man we may imagine.

*

Centuries pass.

Another man's shadow
falls on the rocks.

At once the creatures scatter,
grey seals dive, seabirds
rise clamouring,
even the little warblers,

fellow passengers,
that he loves to glimpse, vanish.

He is alone, in touch
with the earth's crust,
scholar of faults and fractures,
a man launching his mind
on the darkness that surrounds him,
and on the darkness within.

                    *

Where are the poets?
He sniffs the air,
not an ogre, rather
a stag scenting the air
for a rival.

Where are the poets?
Dead with the saints,
with the farmers
and fisher folk?

Is the new language
an air too thin to breathe?

There is an old tongue
that the saints and poets preached,
and the creatures heeded,
and God, perhaps, abided.

Is he, as he stands here
casting his shadow
on the rock, launching
his probes, the last poet?

                    *

Lord, forgive
your poets their pride.

Even the greatest,
the man on the stone beach,
is a frail craft,
a stuttering probe,
an obstructed channel
giving shape to a drop
of the life that made him.

*

Be sure of this.

We have heard his voice.
It will not be unheard.

We have looked with his eyes.
What he has seen
will colour our seeing.

His shadow will remain
on the ancient rocks.
Pilgrims will come
seeking to know his story.

They will imagine him
committing his prayers
to the airways and the waters,
probing the darkness
that is now, because
of him, more nearly their own.

Hurst Castle

'It's very special how there are ways, a field, a place,
where our deepest creative concerns connect.'

Noah Pikes

1
Dear friend,
you have sent my mind racing,
skipping the years.

2
You will know how the sea
runs up among the stones,
how it laps and lapses,
surges with the tide.
And wind whips off the foam.
And the Shingles buoy's bell rings.

Behind us, granite walls,
concrete, brick, rusted steel doors
clamped shut on cannon mouths.

A symbol of power,
once our playground,
empty as a cockle shell.

3
Somehow this place is a way.
I feel I can talk to you through the walls.

4
Remember the Franciscan priest
immured here for thirty years ?

A poor, infirm man, one side
of his body palsied,

how he would shuffle
in a dark, narrow room,
the only human sound
his jailer's tread. Other voices,
the sea's whisper or breaking crash,
a gull's cry.

So news of a far world came to him,
free voices,
which spoke of imprisonment.

5
Who were his brothers then?
And how could he bless?

6
Your voice, dear friend, was choked for years,
unknown as a foreign tongue,
locked in the throat.

At last, released,
it spoke a name that was new to you,
your name,
with a force opening the body's dark and narrow space.

7
You take me back.
So many fields, cities, countries.
And this is the place you bring me to –

This way
of wood and brick defences,
old jetties, the granite castle
with its giant weight of wars
an empty cockle shell.

Words bring me, your words,
words we have spoken to each other,
that connect us to a world.

Outside this narrow room in which I write,
inside, penetrating the walls,
I hear voices that speak of the sea.

from

ANCESTRAL LINES

'Poems are like ghosts, climbing
into one's flesh, when it suits them.'
Andrew Jordan

Canterbury House

1
Harry Mould was his name.

I liked the old man's blue, watery eyes
and kind, domed forehead.

He came alive for me years later
when I heard how much he loved women.

2
He was a picture to me,
the old man – which at a remark –
he loved women –
he strode out of, or I stepped through,
knowing us one flesh.

I returned then
to that house, once so full of life,
which sickness and unhappiness
came to fill, and through it
the man in his vigour walked
driven with longing.

3
The door out of the parlour
led to a treasure house
of junk – old furniture,
musty books, damp mattresses,
a jumble of china oddments.

Things once belonging to the poor
which only the poor buy
or which gather dust, more dust.

Harry, who collected them
had started poor, born in a cottage

on the Hampshire – Wiltshire border.
Adders climbed the thatch –
he feared snakes all his life.

He was a labourer's son
who became a labourer as a boy,
and grew into a man of substance:
a butcher, owner of carts and horses.

During the Great War
his shires were requisitioned
by the Army, and sent to France.

He employed men
to build houses that stand
with his initials under the eaves.

4
Her name was Charlotte.

Lottie, from Bishopstone
under the downland ridge.
She died, leaving him a young family.
It was as if the world ended.

He buried her in a grave
without a headstone,
at Sarisbury Green, where,
long after, he too was buried
in an unmarked grave.

Harry and Lottie,
one common earth,
nothing to say who they were.

Is it pride that makes a man seek
finally to be no one?
Is it humility?

It is, perhaps, one last
gathering of all he is,
and all he loves – the life
beyond all images, that no one can know.

5
What I know my mother told me.
How she loved him
and hated her stepmother.
How she longed for the mother
who had died when she was a child.

It was the place of her memory
that entered me.

I picture it from the outside
with horse-drawn wagons
loaded with strawberries
queueing for the London train.

6
The shed behind the house
had been a stable.
                    I tip-toed in,
keeping close to the door.
Mildewed harness on walls.
Windows hung with cobwebs.

I would like to think I heard
the clop of hooves receding,
gunfire from the distant front.
But there was nothing, only
an absence I would not forget.

7
What is our life
but a river of desire –
                    turbulent,

breaking on shallows,
running deep & dark,
flowing out
with a quick sparkle,
and again, vanishing in shadow.

8
What haunts me is the fact
that everything escapes,

the world of things we touch,
even the beloved's hands.

And what of those
who had no life at all,
James, who lived 10 months,
Charles, who had two weeks.

9
Mother in her last days sat
again at table with the family,
all of them together
before her mother died,
sisters and brother, her father,
Harry, whom she always called Pop.

The house was full of life.

10
To me the place was a door.

It opened on ploughed fields
where the boy turned his ankle
on a ridge, so the man
with a built-up shoe
never walked a straight line.

Behind young Harry Mould
scaring crows, or mixing
a flock of sheep with another
on Stockbridge Down,
I saw the fields falling away,
field upon fields, life upon lives.

Sometimes I know
part of him in my flesh,
and the feel of soil
turning under my shoes.

11
In the photograph
we are all together:
mother and father, brothers,
cousins, uncle and aunt.
The old man too, with that look
of his, kind, watery-eyed.

We are standing
in front of the junkshop
which shows part of his name.

Even now, I can feel
the strain in my flesh
as I pull away
from arms holding me back,
wanting to be free, free.

Cliff-fall house

1
A man walking his dog
might glimpse them passing.

Moonlight silvers waves,
and forms loom, darker in the dark:
breakwaters wreathed with wrack,
emerging or descending.

On the beach
under sand cliffs and slides of clay,
among shingle and shells,
broken brick walls,
a shell of someone's life

and, just visible, young lovers
walking away.

2
We will meet again in dreams
over a lifetime.
Desire unchanging
will fashion changing scenes:

the lyric of being
a mix of memory
and imagined time.

Our initials, J & J
chalked on brick, cut
in wood, but nothing fixed,
invisible signatures
on field and river and wood.

3
Skin to skin
we lie under hazel and oak
or in summer grasses,
eager and awkward
borne on the power
that comes with the sun.

4
We missed each other once.

I crept downstairs,
climbed through the window.
But on the Common, passing
either side of a clump of gorse,
we missed each other in the dark.

I carry this with me
together with a handkerchief
scented and stained with paint
and the first glimpse
of a young art student
wearing a green duffle coat.

5
You sit on the branch of a tree
where I have lifted you,
in your hands sketchbook and charcoal.
All around us, the great field
with the path through June grass,
below, the river valley, an orchard
and the grey tower upstream.

You are drawing what you see.

I see you, and will try
                    to find the words.

6
Sun on sea glitters, shines
on Purbeck and West Wight,
chalk arches of a broken bridge.

On a quiet day we imagine them:
sudden falls and long ages.

Rivers that moulded slowly,
seas that stormed the land,
laying down gravels and sand,
burying ancient life-forms,
bringing fossil beds to light,
inscribing stories of fiercer suns.

Violent rending,
slow accretion, fallings away
and through all
the blood streams,
                    turbulent, dark
shaping new worlds.

7
On a quiet day,
sea calm, sibilant on pebbles
we step down
from fallen gardens,
yellow and mauve lupins
from a border, gone wild
colonise marl and clay
near the sea's edge. Little faces peep
from martin's nests
in the sand and gravel cliff.

The water takes us in.

How cold it is!
Watch for the undertow.
The Island swims
on the horizon, the long shore
shimmers, curves
from Hurst to Hengistbury Head.

Warmer now, our bodies touch.

The sun beats on our heads,
our salt skin shines, we are
one being playing with the sea.

8
It is a glimpse only that he has,
the man walking with his dog;
dark forms looming, breakwaters
emerging or descending,
a little silver that shows the waves,
and young lovers passing
where the broken walls of a house lie
scattered on shingle and sand.

Fairacre

1
Love is first an element,
an atmosphere, a milky cloud

taste & smell & neediness
and then a face, a word.

2
To begin with,
what appears is darkness,
and a dank earthy smell,
mosquitoes whining in my ear.

The blanket I am handed down in
tickles and smells new.
Far off, the crump of bombs –

words I do not know,
but I will learn.

3
I don't know
what I remember,
or remember because I was told.

So I hear the Welsh tenor's voice
as he sings opera by the guns
at night, in Pegrim's field.

4
Called in from digging in the ditch
we watch tanks grinding past
on Greenaway Lane, faces
grinning down at us,
hands throwing gum.

One night tanks parked
in a convoy near Canterbury House
explode, and a brave man
drives his burning tank away
saving others by his act.

It was the spring when Keith Douglas
encamped in the New Forest sent out
soldiers to pick primroses to adorn the tents.

Another brave man, a German
awaiting execution in Germany
writes a letter to the future:

you are learning from childhood
that the world is controlled by forces
against which reason is powerless.

5
Standing on the cinder path
Dave holds me up
and points at the sky.

In crossing beams, a point of light
which, as we watch, disintegrates,
and, like a spent firework, falls
in a shower of stars.

6
Innocently the water flows
picking over remnants
of old forests, old wrecks,
new fragments of ruined lives.

The flow is outward:
Southampton Water
to Solent to Channel
to beaches of Normandy.

My brothers are my heroes.
They swim in the river, dive,
white legs waving in the air.

Among crab shells, weed,
cuttle bone, dogfish egg sacs
the shore is strewn with wreckage
and thick with gobbets of tar.

7
I see a bungalow with a red-tiled roof,
an acre of garden, which my father
did not call fair: *as full of weeds*
as there are devils in hell.

But to me it is fair:
a playground with a laurel hedge
on one side, dense with fleshy leaves
where a blackbird at her nest hides,
and on the other, a strawberry field.

A dozen red hens. A trellis
with one tomato ripening
which I pick, because forbidden.
A sty at the bottom, waiting for a pig.

My father with a garden line
or spade, or hoeing the soil
which is thin and gravelly.

8
I dig with my friend in the ditch,
seeking treasure, and finding stones,
sometimes a fragment of clay pipe,
once a shepherd's crown.

Black-headed gulls cry
as they pass overhead:
voices of the river,
of the sea and its tides,
voices that sound with other voices
in my mind, mixing
with what I remember, what I am told,

fact becoming story,
story becoming myth,
myth becoming part of us,
moulding our lives.

9
Love is first an element,
an atmosphere, a milky cloud.

Out of the cloud a face appears,
and then a word.

from

UNDER THE QUARRY WOODS

Goldfinches on a May morning, feeding on dandelion seeds. Climbing the stems, which occasionally give under them, they settle further down, with a flutter of wings, snatching beakfuls of seed, while other seeds, shaken out, float away on the air. Behind them, at the edge of the woods, new leaves seethe in a breeze, surfaces speckled with light. Strands of spider silk shine. Illuminated seeds float across the garden.

* * *

Fact beggars imagination when I think of Cunarders, *Mauritania & Lusitania,* powered by steam coal from the Deep Navigation, vying for the Blue Riband.

Coal from here lies in *RMS Titanic* on the Atlantic bed.

Here the unseen presses upon the seen, and the ripped land wears a face of unbelievable peace.

* * *

On the path a peacock suns its open wings. Brimstone on a dandelion, yellow bringing out the gold on the whole flower face. A peacock chases off a bee, as a crow would harry a buzzard.

A faint pulse on a small pond. A moth, almost the same colour as mud on the bottom, drowning. Saved with the tip of my stick. But everywhere among the teeming lives are lonely deaths.

Poets make such a fuss of their self-drama, myself not least; but I find that consciousness at its purest and deepest issues in prayer.

* * *

I recall a sort of trance I would sometimes go into, in class, when everything in and around me would become unreal, or change into a new dreamlike reality.

What, then, is strange?

Now, I would say it's the light of a common day: life as we wake into it, from the small self and the world it draws around it. Words have always come to me as provisional, a way of pointing at what is beyond them, at life with a strange identity that is not words. The difference, here, is that my sense of belonging has lifted off, like mist blowing away from the hills. And what is laid bare is the history, the world-transforming movements that changed the landscape, and the way of life they created in the communities, in neighbourhoods that are now ghosts of themselves, with people that are made to feel useless, people who are lost.

Not my history, I could say. But I, as much as anyone, am a product of a transformed world, the society made possible by coal and iron, the wealth of an empire, and what is left behind, which we barely understand. Without the work men and women spent their lives doing here, I wouldn't have been sitting in class in a state of comfortable dreaminess when I was a boy.

Strangeness, then, is also a realisation of connection. Not the idea alone, but the moment when one experiences it, shedding the self's insulation, the isolating carapace.

It is necessarily visitant, like miracle.

It is what I want to break through my words.

* * *

First celandines opening by the brook where morning sun shines full upon them, by quicksilver water.

First daffodils under the beech by the Cannons. Something white caught my eye in the cherry tree. For a hopeful instant it looked like a snowy owl. It was a supermarket carrier bag.

* * *

Robin perched on the Cannon's mouth.

* * *

My son the photographer brings me news.

He cycles into the hills. He walks in desolate tunnels, flashing light in the dark.

He stands on the Giant's Bite, surveying this quarried land of bridges & viaducts, the Taff working its way down to Cardiff and the Bay.

He photographs the Cannons, showing how moss sucks green out of the spectrum.

He reveals the luminous stone.

* * *

One dandelion in the quarry woods, a blazing sunface.

* * *

As yet a faint scent only: bluebells where miners tramped, beside paths where coal dust & cinders are mixed with stones.

* * *

Awake in the night, I remember my first memory. Sirens wail. Loving arms carry me down into cavernous dank, sheltering dark. Strong arms of those long dead.

Owls call to one another in frosty hours. Towards dawn, a ghost of light.

A NOTE ON THE SELECTION

Having made this selection, which has involved revisiting poems written over more than 50 years, and finding that I want to make some statement concerning what my poetry has been about, I realize that I have been moved to write by a sense of the reality of things. These include human making (both the toil of my labouring ancestors, and the work of known and unknown poets and painters), and diverse natural phenomena, such as trees, clouds, birds, flowers, rivers, chalk and sand and flint, the sea and the sea shore. The list is a long one, but it has one common factor: life, the animate and inanimate universe. Late in the day, I borrowed from Henry Vaughan the word that names what I seek: *quickness*. While acknowledging my debt to certain painters, my father not least, I am not primarily a descriptive poet. Early on, in *Soliloquies of a Chalk Giant*, I set out to explore the interaction of creative and destructive powers on which life depends. Years later, in *Under the Quarry Woods*, I expressed what I myself had been seeking: "For a poet or artist to 'make' anything corresponding to nature it's necessary to intimate the stream, the life flowing through the leaf".

From the beginning, I responded keenly to poets who had expressed the spirit of place in my native region in the south of England: Thomas Hardy, Edward Thomas, William Barnes, and Alfred Tennyson. As I've often acknowledged, my principal literary influence was the poet-naturalist Richard Jefferies. Jefferies first taught me to see things I loved, such as the 'common rushes' of 'The Pageant of Summer', and the indescribable colour of the dandelion in 'Nature and Books'. He saw the thing, and he saw the alchemy of nature's processes, and he recognised the limits of his vision. From the commonest natural phenomenon Jefferies takes us to the mysterious heart of the world in which we live. As a boy, I found in Jefferies the kind of emotional perception that was natural to me, and which I came to recognise as a parental gift, from my father's landscape paintings, and my mother's love of nature and poetry.

The nature with which I grew up in the later '40s and '50s, on the edge of the New Forest, with the freedom to roam, was not significantly different on the surface from the Wiltshire of Jefferies and the Hampshire of Edward Thomas. But my first memory was of being carried down into an Anderson shelter during an air raid, and with developing consciousness, especially in my teens, I became aware of living in an endangered world, in which everything and everyone I loved and valued might vanish in a nuclear cataclysm. This meant that I grew up with a protective and defensive attitude towards all that I cared for. My move to Wales in 1965 brought me into contact with a people who felt their culture was being eroded under their feet. These experiences had a profound effect upon my feeling for language. In linguistic terms I was sent back to fundamentals, to the actual things of my first world. In the '70s. I discovered the poetry of the American Objectivists, and felt an immediate affinity with George Oppen's care for the 'little words', for substantives, and naming what we are actually talking about. In my mind, there is a direct link between Oppen's care of words and Wordsworth's statement in 'Essay upon Epitaphs 111': 'Language, if it do not uphold, and feed, and leave in quiet, like the power of gravitation or the air we breathe, is a counter-spirit, unremittingly and noiselessly at work, to subvert, to lay waste, to vitiate, and to dissolve'. A reverential attitude towards nature and the 'common' things of our world links the tradition of *Lyrical Ballads* with that of American poets such as William Carlos Williams, George Oppen and Charles Reznikoff. Henry David Thoreau and Richard Jefferies shared a passion for what the latter called 'coming to have touch of that which is real'.

I am a lyric poet who seeks to free himself from the limitations of a narrow subjectivity. 'Lyric of being', a formulation I arrived at when writing about *Ancestral Lines*, has a bearing on this. The phrase refers to 'the quick of experience, whether felt or glimpsed: the living moment which, in an image, may intimate the whole life it is part of'. At a critical moment, when I was trapped in a solipsistic state of mind, I discovered Martin Buber's philosophy of 'I and Thou' and his conviction that 'all real living is meeting'. Looking back, I recognise that with my early preoccupation with 'belonging and not belonging' I had risked settling for a sense of fixed identity. This was quite contrary to my idea of place not as permanent, settled ground, but as a channel through which life flowed, connecting past and present, the living and the dead. In the '90s, in 'Seven Songs', influenced by Coleridge's and Virginia Woolf's idea of the androgynous imagination, I was seeking to escape the bounds of my male ego. I recognise now that I have been attempting to locate myself as a stranger in relation to the strangeness of being. These are ideas that help me to gain some understanding of myself; they emerge from writing that is largely instinctual.

'Ground' began by meaning to me place in all its constituent elements. With time, it has acquired a meaning that is also metaphysical – in effect, a seeking for common depths, in our relationships with one another, and with the natural world on which our lives depend. It is a word open to other, religious meanings. Openness is what I have sought in all my writings, poetry, journals, and literary criticism. It means writing with a sense of fluid self, of self as process rather than fixed identity, and in relation to a world that is constantly in process. It eschews definitive statements, and perfectly rounded forms, and is not end-stopped. I do not follow American open-field poetry in any doctrinaire way, and David Jones has been more important to me as a breaker of traditional forms than Charles Olson. My idea of openness carries some notion of organic form, but is more concerned with making and breaking of poetic images, in the hope of approaching an ever-elusive reality. Each poem ends with a sense of underlying silence; it is where questions continue, and I hope to find a new beginning. I do not seek mastery over words, or mastery in any form. The powers behind life in this universe, which we can encounter in a wild flower or an earthworm, show us what limited beings we are, and what a danger our pretention to mastery over those powers is. A poetry of relationship seeks to convey a sense of the reality of things.

'Tench Fisher's dawn', first published in 1965, is the earliest poem in this selection. *The Elements,* a pamphlet in the Triskel Poets series, and *Landscape of the Daylight Moon*, represent my beginnings as a published poet, although the latter appeared after *Soliloquies of a Chalk Giant* and in the same year as *Solent Shore*. From early on, I have thought of myself as exploring a 'ground', which for convenience may be thought of as all the elements of a place or region. One consequence of this is that I've tended to write cycles of poems, and book-length sequences, some more closely integrated than others. In certain cases, such as *Soliloquies of a Chalk Giant* and *Solent Shore*, this has made the choice of individual poems especially difficult, since the sequence is a sort of 'conversation' among all the parts. In other instances, notably 'A Winchester Mosaic' and 'From Debris', it has been relatively easy to distinguish between the essential and less essential pieces. What I have sought is to choose poems that can speak for themselves, however closely they may relate to the company they keep. I have excluded from this selection a number of my longer poems, which I felt would be ill represented by selection, although I stand by them as a whole.

ACKNOWLEDGEMENTS

Poems in this selection were first published in:

The Elements (Christopher Davies, 1972)
Soliloquies of a Chalk Giant (Enitharmon Press, 1974)
Solent Shore (Carcanet Press, 1978)
Landscape of the Daylight Moon (Enitharmon Press, 1978)
Englishman's Road (Carcanet Press, 1980)
Master of the Leaping Figures (Enitharmon Press, 1987)
Their Silence a Language (Enitharmon Press, 1993)
Our Lady of Europe (Enitharmon Press, 1997)
Adamah (Enitharmon Press, 2002)
Arnolds Wood (Flarestack, 2005)
The Cut of the Light: Poems 1965-2005 (Enitharmon Press, 2006)
Scattered Light (Enitharmon Press, 2015)
Ancestral Lines (Shearsman Books, 2016)
Under the Quarry Woods (The Pottery Press, 2018)

I am indebted to the publishers of these collections of poetry, and I owe a special debt of gratitude to Michael Schmidt of Carcanet Press, Stephen Stuart-Smith and the late Alan Clodd of Enitharmon Press, Tony Frazer of Shearsman Books, Charles Johnson of Flarestack, and Liz Mathews of The Pottery Press. My thanks are due to Deborah Price for her care in transcribing the text.

Lightning Source UK Ltd.
Milton Keynes UK
UKHW011133280422
402200UK00001B/31